Ta
CAN
Be Taught

The Book on Creating
Music Ability

Foreword by Raymond Aaron
New York Times Top Ten Best Selling Author

Featuring The Powerful PRAISE™ Techniques

Stephen Riches

Contents at a Glance

Author's Acknowledgements

Never for the sake of peace and quiet deny
your own experience or convictions
— **Dag Hammarskjold, Nobel Peace Prize Winner**

In paraphrasing Dag Hammarskjold, it has been said that being willing to state the truth must not be a lower priority than peacekeeping. In every human endeavour, however, improvement can never be accomplished without first challenging existing norms. And, upsetting the status quo is never uneventful, so there will undoubtedly be some who may find some of my statements to be troubling. I, too, have found it disturbing to be continually presented with the evidence of systemlcally poor educational strategies in the area of private music education, even more so because these approaches in general have not been questioned by so many in the profession for as long as I can remember.

Educators take something simple and make it
complicated; communicators take something
complicated and make it simple
— **John C. Maxwell, author**

I believe that it is important to identify educational practices which are long overdue for reform, as well as to communicate clear and constructive proposals for solutions to the many challenges arising from these practices. And, I hope that my book will especially help to motivate parents and teachers to make necessary changes so that the success rate of private music lessons can be improved in future.

In terms of my own personal growth, for many years, I have benefited from the wisdom and experience of many people who dedicated much time and effort planning and presenting practical and motivational strategies for building leaders. In particular, I'd like to thank Raymond Aaron for encouraging me to write this book, as well as for providing the support of his team and even offering to write the Foreword. In addition, I'd like to thank Casey Combden, from whom, along with his many wonderful guest presenters, I learned many valuable lessons, and who regularly taught and inspired me to "dream big and set no limits." And to John Harten of Editworksusa.com, whose help and advice as editor contributed greatly to a project that, as a new author, was very unfamiliar territory for me, as well as to Brandan Stiner who assisted with formatting and creating the logo and book cover, I also owe a special word of thanks

I want to especially acknowledge the support and encouragement that I received from my late mother, Elsie, and my father Albert, both during my years of training, and throughout my career. The sacrifices that they made enabled me to receive music training and develop the music ability with which I've been blessed. I also want to thank my dear wife, Beth, whose own ongoing artistic and administrative support in day to day operations at my studio has been invaluable. Finally, I wish to dedicate the book to our daughter Annelise, whose interest in providing quality music education herself continues a family tradition of respect for the great value and importance of music to a third generation.

Stephen Riches

Foreword
by Raymond Aaron

I first met Stephen about twenty-five years ago when he attended one of my workshops on real estate investing. When we re-acquainted recently, Stephen commented on some things that he had learned from me back then that related to life and human behaviour, and which he had been able to apply countless times over many years of teaching in ways that were helpful to his students.

It is now my pleasure to be able to return the compliment. In recent years, I've witnessed the passion Stephen has about music and teaching. So it comes as no surprise that he would want to write this book to share what he has learned. But passion alone does not create a great book. More important for you is that Stephen demonstrates an understanding of the private music lesson industry, and it is this knowledge that has allowed him to very clearly assess what he refers to as failing traditions. But even better, he also recommends very practical solutions which he has built into a new system for private music education. Add to this a flair for writing and a wonderful ability to organize ideas, quotations, anecdotes, and personal experiences and his book presents information in a very clear, logical, and easy-to-read manner.

Talent CAN Be Taught is one of the finest books that I know on this subject. If you are a teacher or parent and you value excellence in music education, and you want to avoid the difficulties that have caused so many students to give up on their own dreams of having music talent, it is an invaluable resource. Also, if you happen to be one of the countless millions of people who can say that at one time you took private music lessons, you may find that you see yourself, your parents, and your teachers in some of his illustrations. Perhaps most of all you may see yourself in the diagnostic test that he invites you to take at the end of Chapter 3. But perhaps the most exciting part about reading this book is when you come to understand the reasons why you previously became frustrated and perhaps gave up trying to become musically talented, and at the same time realize that with the system Stephen has created it's actually still possible to make it happen.

Stephen has written the book on creating music ability, and now it's ours to enjoy too!

Raymond Aaron – New York Times Top Ten Best Selling Author

Part 1:

Understanding the Challenges of Private Music Education

Chapter 1

Diagnostic Testing

Introduction

Most of this book focuses especially on traditions relating to lessons in piano/keyboard. And, while piano lessons do provide a great foundation for studies in all instruments, most of the principles apply also to the study of music in general, and are transferable to study of other instruments, voice, and theory.

A few years ago, I discovered that traditional approaches to private music lessons have not been serving most students very well. In fact, the problems are not just a recent trend, but rather are part of a much older tradition in existence for decades. The details of this tradition are multi-faceted, but there are certain common forces involved that create challenges that are occurring with increasing frequency.

By way of introducing some of the key points that are at work here, I am reminded of a great classic novel which I read as a young person. *Tom Sawyer*, by American author Mark Twain (Samuel Clemens), was one of my favourite books in my pre-teen years. Two episodes in particular from this novel came to mind as I've recently been coming face to face with challenges that today's students are facing. These challenges have provided the inspiration for my book. The premise, as my book title indicates is that it is possible to create musical ability. Unfortunately, all too often, that's not what happens.

The following two episodes from *Tom Sawyer* will help serve as an introduction to the culture or societal thinking that is actually becoming a road-block to the creation of musical ability.

Two Episodes in the Life of Tom Sawyer

The two episodes to which I've referred are directly linked. The first is the famous account in Chapter Two where Tom has been banished by his Aunt Polly to whitewash the fence on Saturday morning as a punishment for skipping school and going swimming at the local watering hole with some other boys the previous afternoon. Tom uses psychology to get the boys of the village to consider that whitewashing the fence is a special privilege, since it isn't an everyday event. Further, he suggests that it requires a certain amount of skill that not everyone has. To complement his strategy, he does not easily give in when his friends begin to beg for a turn at doing the work. Eventually, however, as Mark Twain puts it, "he gives up the brush with reluctance on his face, but alacrity in his heart." Tom's strategy works so well that his friends line up to sacrifice all of their worldly wealth of odds and ends to him for the privilege of painting this fence in the burning heat of the day. Meanwhile, Tom sits relaxing in the shade, and accepts payments for the privilege of whitewashing, and the fence gets whitewashed several times over. His Aunt has no idea how greatly her intended punishment has actually benefitted her entrepreneurial nephew. Meanwhile, Tom takes credit for work which he has not done, and basks undeservedly in his Aunt's approval.

The second episode takes place the very next day (on Sunday morning). Having to dress up for church, and especially wear shoes, is a torturous experience for Tom exceeded only by having to try to memorize Bible verses each week. Ever seeking the easy way out, this time he settles on the Sermon on the Mount, after much research, because of its repetitive nature and overall brevity (with so many short verses beginning with the words "Blessed are...."). However, Tom has a crush on a new girl at school named Becky, which proves to be a source of inspiration for him. She is the daughter of an auspicious new resident in the community, Judge Thatcher, who is going to be attending church with his family on this occasion. And, like so many others attending church that day, Tom wants to "show off." The Superintendent's own plan to show off is to try to find a great "prodigy" to whom he can give an award for memorizing Bible verses. The ultimate prize is a Bible to be awarded for memorizing two thousand verses. Students receive a blue ticket for memorizing two verses. Ten blue tickets could be exchanged for one red ticket, and 10 red tickets for a yellow ticket. Ten yellow tickets, representing the memorization of 2000 verses, would make the holder eligible to be awarded a Bible.

So Tom sets to work, but not memorizing verses. He takes the wealth that he has accumulated by allowing his friends to whitewash the fence the day before, and sells it back to them in exchange for their blue, yellow, and red tickets. And just when the Superintendent is despairing that there isn't going to be a single student able to claim the prize, since none has any more than three yellow tickets, Tom appears before the Superintendent in view of all present. He is holding 9 yellow tickets, 9 red tickets, and 10 blue ones, the required number for the award, anticipating that the praise heaped upon him will endear him to Becky Thatcher. Unfortunately, however, Tom's glory is very short-lived. The gig is up when he is introduced to Judge Thatcher who asks him to display some of his amazing Bible knowledge by answering a skill-testing question; specifically, the names of just two of Jesus' disciples.

Of course, and unfortunately for Tom, he has no Bible knowledge whatsoever. In fact, the only names from the Bible that he can remember are "David" and "Goliath." One is left to imagine the reaction of all present, as the author simply brings the chapter to a close with the words, "Let us draw the curtain of charity on the rest of the scene."

Summary of the Episodes from Tom Sawyer

The embarrassment for Tom and those in the church that day who had hoped to display a young prodigy to the judge, centred on the fact that although Tom presents evidence that suggests that he has learned two thousand verses, he hadn't actually learned any verses at all. In fact, his actual knowledge of the Bible is almost non-existent. So, in effect, he is fraudulently presenting the coloured tickets for personal gain. I remember admiring Tom's commitment to chasing his dream (his pursuit of Becky Thatcher), as well as smiling at the irony that he is able to trick the other boys of the village and achieve something for nothing not once, but twice. And, to a certain extent, inasmuch as we all may sometimes cheer for the underdog, I also admired his ingenuity in "beating the system," (which in this case set such a high standard that almost nobody would be able to win the award), by managing to acquire the tickets without actually doing any of the work. All the while, however, even as a young person, I understood that somehow the whole purpose of the contest and the awarding of tickets for memorization of verses, which was an admirable goal, had been subverted by Tom. And, in the end his highly enterprising but completely misguided efforts fail him most of all.

The key point that I wish to make here, is that in both cases, Tom's evidence was fraudulent. He does not serve his aunt's punishment for skipping school, and he does not memorize the Bible verses, despite the evidence that he presents. In short, Tom's evidence was a misrepresentation of the truth, and the diagnostic test, which in Tom's case came in the form of a skill-testing question, revealed this fact.

Tom Sawyer at Work in Private Music Education

This same strategy is being used in the accumulation of RCM certificates by numerous parents and students, apparently, in many cases, with the willingness, if not entirely the approval, of their teachers.

Some years ago, I offered my services to teach private lessons at a very large music studio that had numerous franchises. I worked at two of the largest of these franchises that, combined, had more than 2000 students taking lessons every week. Because my qualifications were considerably more extensive than other teachers who worked there, the plan of the owner was to assign the more senior students to me. However, during these several years when I taught at these two studios as many as four or five evenings a week, almost all of my students were Pre-Grade One level students in their first few years of having lessons. The only time, in fact, that I actually heard music of a somewhat more advanced level being played in one of the studios, I discovered, on investigating, that it was being played by another teacher. Altogether, during the several years of teaching at this studio, I only ever had two piano students who were even attempting moderately advanced levels. One was studying at the Grade 5 RCM level, and another was assigned to me to begin study at the Grade 8 RCM level.

The experience that I had with the Grade 8 student at this school in particular, and for which I will provide additional details later, is similar to some that I have had with other students since. Together, these became the inspiration for developing a better private music education system, as well as for the writing of this book.

The First Lesson and a Diagnostic Test

It is always very important when beginning to work with a student who has taken lessons previously to perform a diagnostic test to determine the level of development of the new student's music skills. It is not enough to simply take the student's word for the level that they have achieved and/or the level that they or their parents have indicated that they plan to start working toward achieving. A good educational plan must take into account areas of both strength and weakness, and take steps to address personal needs. Complicating matters, and another reason that careful testing is required, is that some parents actually switch teachers for the purpose of skipping levels of study as well as to try to impose demands or limitations relating to the course of study to be followed. And, very frequently, the students' own musical limitations make parent demands very unrealistic.

Sometimes in such situations, parents may also be unwilling to provide evidence in the form of examiner's reports, which, if provided, help a new teacher to diagnose a student's specific needs. Sometimes, my own diagnostic testing reveals that the student is performing far below the level that the parent has claimed. However, often true diagnostic testing by the teacher in order to make a professional determination of what the student really needs, is replaced by following a parent's request for the course of study to be followed by the student.

Most of the dialogue between teacher and student that follows was taken from my first meeting with the prospective Grade 8 RCM student, while a few of the details are composites of other similar situations since then. This exchange is a pattern that I've found to be occurring regularly.

A First Meeting Between Teacher and Student

Teacher (to new student asking to study Grade 8 Piano) – Congratulations on Grade 7
Student – I didn't do Grade 7.
Teacher – Oh, I'm sorry. What was the last exam level that you completed?
Student – Grade 5.
Teacher – Really? Well, perhaps we should spend some time on Grade 6 first.
Student – My mom wants me to get a Grade 8 certificate for a high school credit.
Teacher – Oh. Well, congratulations on Grade 5. By the way, what was your exam mark?
Student – I can't remember.
Teacher – Well, did you receive Honours, or First Class Honours on the examiner's report?
Student – I don't know where the report is. I think it was just a pass.
Teacher – Did you find some parts of the exam difficult?
Student – Yes.
Teacher – Well, play something for me now?
Student – I can't.
Teacher – Do you like to play anything just for fun?
Student – No.
Teacher – Well, why don't you just play one of your Grade 5 exam pieces?
Student – I can't remember any.
Teacher – Well, when did you take the Grade 5 exam?
Student – Last June
Teacher – That's just a few months ago. Can't you play even one of them?
Student – No.
Teacher – Well, when was the last time you played any of the exam pieces?
Student – At the exam.
Teacher – Well, open up your music book and see if you can remember one of them.
Student – I don't have the book. It belonged to my other teacher.
Teacher – No problem, I have one here. Do you recognize any of these pieces?
Student – (after a long search) – I think I learned this one.
Teacher – OK. Try that one, then.
Student – (starts to play with the right hand only, with many note and rhythm errors).
Teacher – (substituting a Pre-Grade 1 level book) – Let's try some sight reading.

Summary and Interpretation of the Diagnostic Test

The student in the above example then struggles through a novice Pre-Grade 1 level selection. After a few minutes and numerous errors, he manages to get through the sixteen very basic bars of music at this level, playing one hand and one note at a time, in a very basic introductory position on the keyboard. The piece happens to finish on Middle C, which is usually the first note that students ever learn to play and the first one that they are taught to recognize, both on the music page, and on the piano keyboard. Turning the page, I ask the student to try the next selection. This selection happens to begin on Middle C, which is the very same note that the student just finished playing on the previous page. The student however, doesn't seem to recognize it, but stares at the music page at length, trying to figure out where to put his hands.

At this point, like Mark Twain, I also "draw the curtain of charity on this scene" and cease tormenting the student by not continuing to ask him to demonstrate these novice level music skills any more. Instead, I begin to consider the reality that it is necessary for me to first explain to the parents that the student isn't ready for Grade 8. Secondly, as this diagnostic test revealed, I have to also explain that the student really isn't even demonstrating skills in keeping with the Grade 5 level that he is reported to have already completed. I also repeat my request for the supporting evidence of an RCM examiner's report. With persistence, the examiner's report is sometimes eventually produced, then confirming what is evident from the diagnostic test; namely that there are significant areas of weakness which will severely impede further progress unless a lot of time is spent on review.

When Certificates Don't Equal Achievement of Skills

In this example, which is typical of a growing number of examples, a student whose mother intends that he begin study of Grade 8 RCM piano cannot actually play anything at all from the last Grade level taken (Grade 5). Even more unfortunately, the student also struggles to read music at a Pre-Grade 1 level (RCM Preparatory A Level).

So why is it that there are students and parents who are seeking to begin piano studies at the Grade 8 level without first having developed the skills to even read music competently at a basic Preparatory A or novice level? Or, perhaps more to the point, who is to blame for this situation?

Who Is to Blame for Student Failures?

The Royal Conservatory of Music is not responsible for the abuse of carefully developed standards by parents, students and teachers who want to obtain certificates without developing their skills, any more than the Sunday school superintendent was responsible for Tom's circumventing the intent of the contest by purchasing tickets from other students. The RCM is very dedicated to establishing standards of testing that are designed to accurately measure student achievements.

Neither are public school boards to blame simply because they offer a credit to high school students to honour the achievement and skill development that Grade 7 and 8 RCM certificates are intended to represent.

Further, even the music student cannot be held responsible for parents who try to take short-cuts, or for teachers who fail to exercise good professional judgment. And it is certainly very unfair to blame the student for a lack of progress or significant areas of weakness with suggestions that the student doesn't practice enough or lacks sufficient talent.

The problem is a systemic one that has been created by parents and teachers who in many cases agree to work together to defeat the system. Of course, they may not actually see themselves as defeating the system. But the plans that are implemented at the request of the parent, and with the compliance if not actually the blessing of the teacher, lead to accomplishing exactly that.

Parents, Teachers, and a Failing Tradition

Ultimate responsibility or blame must rest with those who either manipulate the system or allow it to be manipulated by taking short-cuts to achieve certificates that fail to accurately represent what the student has really learned. Like Tom Sawyer, there are always some people who will work overtime at trying to create these short-cuts. And, while the student usually takes the blame for failures, there are many clear indicators that teachers and parents must share responsibility, as will be explained in Chapter 3.

The Parent Trap

The quick answer about why the system is being abused is that some parents want their children to receive Grade 7 and 8 RCM certificates which then can be used as a credit toward a high school diploma. And they want to acquire these certificates as quickly as possible, with as few lessons as possible, and with the least amount of effort and expense as possible. In fact, whether or not the student is able to develop any usable music skills is a much lower priority, if, in fact, there is any desire at all to acquire the actual skills. By setting out to receive these certificates, they are endorsing the Tom Sawyer school of learning. They plan to present metaphorical coloured tickets in order to qualify for a high school credit, no matter how meaningless the achievement. Parents, then, are trapped by their own misguided ideas about the value of education in general, and the real purpose of certificates of achievement and school credits in particular.

The Teacher Bait

But a more complete answer to the question about who is responsible for student failures is that many teachers must share some responsibility. Teachers are facilitating the abuse of the system by allowing parents to dictate what should solely be a teacher's professional duty and decision. Fear that the parents will go to another teacher is certainly an influencing factor. And most parents may be unable to truly evaluate the quality of the education that they are receiving or the importance of recommendations that are being made. So issues such as cost, convenience, and teacher co-operation often rule the day.

There is nothing in the world that some man cannot make a little worse and sell a little cheaper, and he who considers price only is that man's lawful prey. – John Ruskin

Parents bait their own trap by making it clear that if the teacher is not willing to do what they want, they will go elsewhere to find one who may perhaps even give lessons at a lower cost or provide them more conveniently. Anxious not to lose the potential income, most teachers simply comply with parent demands for an ill-advised educational plan.

The Bigger Picture

Problems arising from parent demands, combined with teacher reluctance to insist on doing what is best for the student for fear of losing the client altogether, are in some cases even compounded by teaching deficiencies. These are signs of a systemic problem, rather than a few isolated cases.

The most common and widely accepted practices associated with teaching music privately are part of, and responsible for, a number of the failing traditions that have been in practice for many decades. These traditions continue to persist to the present day, despite almost a 100% failure rate (student dropout rate) over an average period of a few months to a few years. Even those students who persist to more advanced levels, as illustrated by the above example of the first meeting between teacher and student, and who diligently strive to survive despite an agonizingly slow learning process, have very major weaknesses in their actual music skills. Very few get as far as the student in this example, because trying to learn without having the necessary reading and ear training skills becomes a very painfully slow and tedious process.

A detailed list of signs of "Failing Traditions" is the subject of Chapter 3. But before we explore the nature and causes of these failing traditions, however, it is important to take time to understand what is meant by the word "talent," and how music ability can be created. To do so, we need to begin by exploring the connection between music talent and music skills, after which we will be better able to understand the role of The Powerful PRAISE Techniques in creating music ability.

Please visit: www.talentcanbetaught.com

Chapter 2:

Understanding Talent and Skill Set

The younger kids have the most musical chops—not because they have some musical gene, but because they grow up in a musical hothouse, filled with models, visions of who they might become. Simply put, they have more fuel.
– Daniel Coyle

In his book, *The Talent Code*, author Daniel Coyle comments on something which he refers to as "the Michael Jackson syndrome." Just as Michael Jackson, being the youngest of his very musical family, became the star musician of the family, he sees a pattern of extraordinary achievement often hy the youngest family members resulting from a thorough exposure to a musical environment.

Is talent primarily a factor of environment?

One of the greatest of musical talents of all time was the Austrian composer Wolfgang Amadeus Mozart. The stories of his enormous talent at a very early age are legendary. His father, Leopold, was a highly respected professional musician who also composed music. It is well-known that, like Michael Jackson, young Mozart was exposed to music from a very early age, and was taught both piano and violin by his father. But was his great talent the result of his environment, which included regular exposure to music from the time he was born (or perhaps even before he was born), or was it the result of his genetic heritage? Many might argue in favour of one or another. Some might even say that it was a little bit of both, and perhaps this is true. In *The Talent Code*, Daniel Coyle similarly references Mozart as an example of one who was exposed to a highly musical environment. He also gives the example of young Emily Bear, who is a Mozart-like prodigy in the Midwest USA thriving in a musical environment which includes having a grandmother who is a concert pianist.

Does talent tend to be associated with speed of learning and youth?

It may not be possible to disentangle whether environment or heredity has a greater influence on musical talent.   But perhaps a more interesting question, has to do with whether or not we perceive talent to be associated with speed of learning and youth, as is the case with Emily Bear, and as was also the case with Mozart.   More information on Emily Bear's amazing talent is available at the links below.

http://en.wikipedia.org/wiki/Emily_Bear

http://www.bing.com/videos/search?q=emily+bear

What is clear is that Mozart displayed superior music skills from a very young age, as does young Emily.   From the age of about six, Mozart travelled with his father throughout Europe, performing on both the piano and violin, and was widely recognized as having an amazing talent. In fact, incredibly, by this age also, he had actually begun composing music of a fairly sophisticated quality.

So was Mozart perhaps considered talented because he was so young, and because he had learned so quickly?   And if this is true, then does it follow that someone who is older or who learns more slowly is somehow less talented, even if they eventually demonstrate the very same skills? Or, to put this another way, we might ask if both young and old alike should be considered equally talented if they are able to display the same music skills, in which case, is there really any difference between talent and skill set?

Are both heredity and environment needed to develop music talent?

As the son of a talented musician, Mozart potentially was pre-disposed genetically for musical talent.   But at the same time, he was both exposed to music and trained in music from a very early age.   So he clearly also benefited from living in an extremely musical environment.

But are both heredity and environment needed to develop musical talent? History shows that there have been many examples of very talented musicians who were not born into a musical family, and likewise many examples of children born to musicians who did not follow in their parents' footsteps, despite having, presumably, the advantages of both heredity and environment.

Is either genetics or environment more important than the other?

Also, can either genetics or environment be considered to be more important than the other?   Canadian conductor, Boris Brott comes from a very musical family.   His father, Alexander, was a violinist and composer, and his mother, Lotte, was a cellist, while his brother, Denis, is also a well-known professional cellist.   And, there are countless other examples of great musical talent running in families. But is the reason for the great musical talent of Boris and Denis the result of genetics or environment?

"Greatness isn't born. It's Grown" – Daniel Coyle

Scientific studies have also shown that a musical environment can actually begin before birth.   According to Dr. Norman Weinberger, professor of neurobiology and behaviour, "not only can music be learned in utero but it can also be remembered after birth." This quotation from his book, *Lessons of the Music Womb, 1999*, along with numerous other examples of the role of environment in pre-natal learning, can be found in an article at the following link:

http://birthfaith.org/mothering/prenatal-music-exposure

In the cases of Boris and Denis Brott, as with Michael Jackson, Wolfgang Mozart, Emily Bear, and many more families that many of us could cite, the lines between a musical heritage and a musical environment may not be very clear. In all of these cases, undoubtedly both environmental and hereditary factors are present, but to determine which most impacted the skill development of the young person would be very difficult.   In my own case, neither of my parents had developed musical talent, although both of them did enjoy music, and from an early age exposed me to it regularly. So environment was certainly a very important factor in my own musical development.

What really matters?

What is clear is that regardless of how much of a role heredity may have in pre-disposing someone to the potential for developing music talent, it is evident that music talent can be a product of environment, if it does not, in fact, absolutely require certain environmental conditions. And so, regardless of whether or not a genetic heritage is involved, talent is something that can be acquired through exposure to a musical environment. In other words, music ability is something that can be created---talent can be taught.

Summary

I think it is also important to understand what is meant by the terms "talent" and "skill set." When it comes to education, knowledge, although important, has very limited value on its own. Music education is ultimately about practical skill development or *applied* knowledge, rather than simply information or *theoretical* knowledge. And so, the primary goal of music lessons is to develop talent which is displayed through practical, demonstrable performance skills.

Talent and Skill Set are synonymous; a display of talent is likewise a display of acquired skills, and a person who displays music skills has music talent.

So, as a premise for this book, talent and skill set should be considered to be synonymous, where a display of talent is a display of acquired skills, and a person who displays music skills is likewise said to be talented. In the chapters that follow, we will see exactly *how* Talent CAN Be Taught.

Please Visit: www.talentcanbetaught.com

Chapter 3:

Recognizing the Signs of "Failing Traditions"

What do I mean by "failing traditions?" What are these traditions, and how and why have they failed? Before we take a detailed look at the process of developing talent, it is helpful to understand why so many have failed to develop it. And because the premise of the book is that Talent CAN Be Taught, or, in other words, music ability can be created, then it is important also to understand why in so many cases, talent has *not* been taught...music ability has *not* been created.

During my years of studying Music Education in University, I became aware of an attitude shared by some students in the Performance department toward those who chose Music Education that was summed up by the old adage that "those who can perform do so; and those who cannot perform, just teach." At the time, as someone who never hesitated to perform when the occasion presented itself, but at the same time loved to teach, I considered this attitude to be rather arrogant. But over the years, I have discovered that it is not without foundation. In fact, it is less often the exception than the rule.

But to say that private music instruction is compromised by failing traditions still requires some explanation. In particular, it is reasonable to ask what the signs of these failing traditions are. The following fifteen traditions represent some of the most frequently occurring indicators of failure which I have encountered.

Tradition #1 – A High Dropout Rate

Millions of people in North America who are living today took private music lessons at some time in the past, usually for a few months or years. But after a while, they became frustrated and quit, assuming that they didn't have talent, and the system depends upon the mistaken idea that a lack of innate talent is the determining factor that explains this statistic. As many as 99% of all private music students are still quitting after just a few months or years of lessons, and soon are unable to demonstrate any music skills at all, despite many hundreds if not even thousands of dollars per student having been spent on private lessons.

Almost all students become discouraged and quit. They are victims of a system that blames lack of innate talent for a statistical failure rate that is unacceptable in any other educational discipline.

Tradition #2 – Where Are the Basic Music Skills?

A few students and parents do persist despite the difficulties they experience, and many students may even get RCM certificates, without actually developing the skills that the certificates are intended to represent. Most students also don't learn to read music notation beyond the most basic level of identifying lines and spaces, nor do they learn to play by ear, yet these two abilities are the two most important and fundamentally basic of all music skills. Due to these deficiencies, learning pieces for RCM exams is so very time consuming that performance technical skills are also neglected.

Many students fail to develop even the most basic of music skills.

Tradition #3 – Goal Setting

Many students skip grade levels and skip parts of standard music curricula in a quest to get to a higher certification level sooner. In fact, their goal, in the first place, is often simply for a certificate, rather than for the actual music skills. This ambition to acquire certificates rather than skills, together with the resulting short-cuts that are commonly taken, causes major gaps in learning.

Many teachers do not work with students and parents to establish appropriate goals for success.

Tradition #4 – Limited Exposure to Music Repertoire

Many students only learn three pieces and one or two studies each year when following these failing traditions. Their sole purpose in learning this music is to take an RCM exam, after which, they have no intention to ever play those pieces again as long as they live.

Due to very limited exposure to repertoire, many students do not learn the important basics of musical style which are essential to success in more advanced-level RCM exams.

Tradition #5 – Misuse of Curriculum Materials

Most private teachers don't follow through with all levels and materials in a comprehensive and sequential curriculum, but take shortcuts that jeopardize a solid foundation for learning. Some curriculum books are skipped, some selections are skipped within the books, and some levels of the curriculum are skipped altogether. So, the end result, as might be expected, is huge gaps in learning.   Few teachers, if any, keep a daybook to track steps in learning.

Using inferior curriculum materials, and compromising the use of well-designed materials always leads to poorly-developed reading skills.   It also creates a learning experience that becomes slower and more frustrating with each level of advancement.   Many students working at levels as high as RCM Grade 8, and who have been victims of this tradition, cannot read music notation satisfactorily at much above a beginner or novice level.

Many independent private teachers use an unplanned approach to the use of curriculum materials, and as a result, many important music concepts are not even taught.

Typically, after a very brief time spent in an introductory curriculum, and learning only a few of the basics, many students are being plunged by their teachers into a Grade 1 or 2 conservatory level book where they learn only 3 pieces and a study for their first exam.   As a result, the necessary foundation and comprehensive understanding of basic music symbols, terms, and important concepts as well as technical aspects of performing is lacking.

Tradition #6 – Poor Teaching Strategies

In an effort to try to help students to read music notation, many private teachers ironically use strategies that actually prevent students from improving their reading skills, such as writing letter names under notes.

Many independent private music teachers use ineffective teaching strategies.

Tradition #7 – Monitoring versus Teaching

While using poor strategies or not using effective ones is a problem, some private teachers actually don't even teach at all, but rather simply monitor student progress and assign work for the student to learn through independent practice. In some cases, teachers cannot perform pieces they are assigning to their students, have poorly developed musical ears, and do not read music well themselves. As a result, they sometimes don't even recognize some of the most basic errors of rhythm or note that are being made by their students.

Some independent private music teachers really do not even teach their students at all.

Tradition #8 – Blaming Students For Failures

Many teachers blame slow student progress on either a lack of talent or a lack of practice, rather than recognizing that more often than not, student failures are the result of ineffective teaching strategies.

Too many independent private music teachers blame students for lack of success.

Tradition #9 – Lack of Teacher Supervision & Training

Most private teachers are completely independent and therefore have no professional supervision, nor do they have any plans for their own professional development or personal growth, either as a musician in general, or as a teacher in particular. They often have significant weaknesses themselves, and invariably, they pass on their own weaknesses to their students.

No independent private music teachers, by definition, have any supervision at all, and most also have no plans to engage in any professional development activities.

Tradition #10 – "A Picture's Worth Ten Thousand Words"

Not only do most private teachers not perform personally in public, but they don't even demonstrate to their students how particular pieces should be performed from a stylistic standpoint. And, no student can learn about style by having someone tell them how to do it; it must be demonstrated.

Few teachers demonstrate for their students, which is the single most effective of all teaching tools.

Tradition #11 – Bad Habits and Practice Methods

Many independent private music teachers allow their students to form bad habits and do not insist on using proven successful strategies for learning, such as emphasizing rhythmic accuracy, regular review of old repertoire, providing opportunities for performance, teaching students how to practice, or requiring students to play slowly and steadily when learning new selections.

Many independent private music teachers allow their students to develop bad habits which impede their progress.

Tradition #12 – No Intent for Review

Many students, despite receiving RCM certificates of achievement, cannot perform a single piece that they have ever learned, either by memory, or using the printed music, because they never review any of the music they've learned after the day of the RCM exam.

Many students are unable to perform any of the pieces that they have ever learned.

Tradition #13 – Undeveloped Synergy of Learning

The traditional formula of taking one half-hour private lesson per week is destined to fail most students, as would having that minimal amount of expert support in any other course of study.

Students don't experience any synergy or motivation from accelerated learning due to a very minimal lesson schedule.

Tradition #14 – Unaddressed Weaknesses

Even when corrective measures are recommended, parents and students often strenuously resist these efforts, due to the perception that learning will be slower or because review of past levels of study creates an impression that the student is not progressing. Sometimes in life, however, it is necessary to retreat for a short time, for a period of re-grouping, in order to be able to move forward more efficiently, quickly, and successfully. Such proven strategies, however, are often not welcomed by parents and students whose goal is merely to achieve certificates as quickly and cheaply as possible.

Critical weaknesses are not addressed before attempting to progress further

Tradition #15 – The Ultimate Failing Tradition

Students who survive this system and who may even get certificates that indicate that they've obtained a level of music skill development that is much higher than that which they have actually acquired, then often use their accreditation to promote themselves as skilled teachers, thereby getting paid as independent private teachers to continue this failing tradition.

Studying with these teachers
at any price
is far too high a price to pay.

Summary of the "Failing Traditions"

The traditions that I have described are common and widespread experiences of students who have studied with private independent music teachers. Many teachers have limited qualifications, and even some who are qualified do not use proven successful strategies for learning. All independent private teachers are unsupervised and so have no professional guidance. Most teachers have some areas of weakness, but few independent private teachers have any plans at all for their own professional development. Nor, often, do they even strategically and thoroughly follow a sequential and comprehensive curriculum that could help to eliminate their shortcomings. And since students who have come up through this tradition become private teachers themselves, it is entirely understandable why rates of student success have been extremely low for many decades.

The above examples are only some of the most frequent of traditions that are failing music students everywhere. These failing traditions have developed primarily as a result of a shift in thinking. In many cases, the goal for many in taking music lessons for many years now has not been to develop music skills that can be used in many varied music fields, including teaching, but rather to simply acquire a certificate which may be applied as a credit toward a high school diploma or be used as a promotional tool for employment. It is the product of an era when mis-representing achievements, having instant gratification and developing a sense of entitlement have become acceptable ways of thinking, while respect for attributes such as diligence, integrity, acquiring useful skills, and making a positive contribution to society are seen as less important, if they are actually valued at all. Sadly, this strategy of achieving certificates without acquiring the intended music skills that they are intended to represent has over the years increased both the rate and the degree of incompetence both among the teachers and their students. This trend can be changed for the better simply by using a better training system and this opportunity exists for people of all ages.

The Style Factor

There's one more point that relates to Tradition #4. I indicated that lack of exposure to repertoire meant that students were not learning about style. But another reason for a lack of understanding of style is that most students don't listen to good examples of a variety of styles of music. And without its characteristic style, which must be an important component of music studies, a tune from any genre of music, whether it be classical, jazz, gospel, rock, reggae, or any other, ceases to really represent that genre. Further, if the distinctive characteristics of two different styles of music are not understood, there is a danger that both could be played the same way, or the wrong way. All music should not be played the same way, and a great performance always captures the style of the genre, which is found in the style of a particular place and time, as well as in an individual composer or artist's personal style. Without stylistic differences, all music would sound the same.

Beethoven
sounds like
Bach
sounds like
Bachman
sounds like
Brubeck
sounds like
Billy Joel
sounds like
Bob Marley
sounds like
The Beatles
sounds like
Beyonce

In the famous coda to the reprinting of his novel *Fahrenheit 451*, the great science fiction writer Ray Bradbury noted the effect of removing style on the works of great writers, because the only way that any single collection of writings could include hundreds of stories is if all of the most important and distinctive aspects of a writer's style were to be eliminated. In effect, to create such huge anthologies, stories would have to be "censored" which just happened to be the very subject of the aforementioned novel. In fact, Bradbury had been inspired to write this story about a futuristic society that censored books, at least in part, because of the Nazi book burnings. His lifelong passionate opposition to all those who wanted to impose censorship on him and other writers is evident in the following excerpt from an essay that he wrote on this subject many years after his book had first been printed.

Incidentally, it is noteworthy, as well as highly ironic that even this novel on the theme of censorship had itself been censored to remove rough language. The following excerpt from his essay highlights an important problem, not only for authors of books, but also composers of music.

Excerpt from "The Coda" for Fahrenheit 451

Some five years back, the editors of yet another anthology for school readers put together a volume with some 400 (count 'em) short stories in it. How do you cram 400 short stories by Twain, Irving, Poe, Maupassant and Bierce into one book? Simplicity itself. Skin, debone, demarrow, scarify, melt, render down and destroy. Every adjective that counted, every verb that moved, every metaphor that weighed more than a mosquito - out! Every simile that would have made a sub-moron's mouth twitch - gone! Any aside that explained the two-bit philosophy of a first-rate writer - lost! Every story, slenderized, starved, bluepenciled, leeched and bled white, resembled every other story. Twain read like Poe read like Shakespeare read like Dostoevsky read like - in the finale - Edgar Guest. Every word of more than three syllables had been razored. Every image that demanded so much as one instant's attention - shot dead...The point is obvious. There is more than one way to burn a book. And the world is full of people running about with lit matches.

– Ray Bradbury

Bradbury's passion is justified.   Eliminating a composer's style or eliminating the characteristic style of a particular time and place is also a form of censorship.   That is not to say, of course, that new, different, and equally wonderful music creations cannot be based on compositions from the past and performed in an entirely different style.   But diminishing a performance because of a lack of understanding of how the piece should be played is unfortunate, and learning about music style characteristics must be considered an essential part of music instruction.   Otherwise, in this adapted paraphrase of Ray Bradbury's essay, Beethoven will sound like Bach will sound like Bachman will sound like Brubeck will sound like Billy Joel will sound like Bob Marley will sound like The Beatles will sound like Beyonce.   And when that happens, all music is diminished.

You may wish to check out Bradbury's inspiring, humorous, and very passionately emphatic essay on this topic in its entirety at the following link:

http://www.angelfire.com/ga/page451/raybradbury.html

Choose to Be Successful

Choosing to place the proper emphasis on actually developing music ability is a decision. If you are a parent who took lessons briefly as a child but have very little to show for it, and regret not having music ability, you may want to avoid the same pitfalls with your children that you encountered in your own personal experience. And if you are like many adults, you may even decide to start again and do it right. In either case, as you continue through this book, you should get a sense of renewed hope, because you will learn how talent can be taught.

A Short Survey

Here is a survey that you can take very quickly to determine if you may be a victim of one or more of these failing traditions, if you have not already figured this out. Perhaps you yourself experienced one or more of the fifteen signs of failing traditions that I included in this chapter. If you are one of the millions of people described in Tradition #1, who once had private music lessons, but quit after a very short time, which is perhaps the most universal of all of the symptoms, how many of the other fourteen failing traditions did you also personally experience, and which may likely have been a contributing factor in your decision or your parents decision that you should quit taking lessons?

Survey Part A

1   During the time that you had music lessons, did you learn to read music notation?
2   Did you learn to play music by ear?
3   Did you learn or were you taught how to practice?
4   Did you develop the ability to learn a page of music in about ten minutes?
5   Did you memorize any pieces of music during the time that you took private lessons?
6   Did you perform pieces publicly that you learned during the time that you took private lessons?
7   Did you learn the characteristic features of different musical styles and periods of music history?

Survey Part B

1   Have you forgotten how to play most or all of the pieces that you ever learned?
2   Did you spend many months learning just a very few pieces?
3   Did you ever skip books or grade levels to try to advance more quickly?
4   Did you feel frustrated when trying to practice on your own?
5   Did you get just one half-hour private lesson per week at most?
6   Did your teacher allow you to write letter names under the notes on the music page?
7   Since you quit taking lessons, have you believed that you lacked music talent?

Answer Key for the Survey

In a successful educational tradition,
all of the answers to Part A would be YES

In a successful educational tradition,
all of the answers to Part B would be NO

What Are the Signs
of a Successful Music Tradition?

A Personal Creed

*Those who develop skills in a successful music tradition,
do not quit,
but progress to a very advanced level.*

*They enjoy good reading skills,
and a well-trained musical ear
that enables them to learn new music quickly by either method.*

*They know and are able to perform by memory,
and with stylistic awareness,
hundreds of pieces of music for their own personal enjoyment.*

*They also share their skills publicly,
either as a teacher,
or by performing for the benefit of others,
in keeping with the very fundamental nature and purpose of music.*

Interpreting the Results of the Test

The above statement about the signs of a successful music tradition is an unofficial creed and mission statement for The Talent CAN Be Taught System™. If most of your answers on the survey were opposite to the Answer Key, meaning that you were a victim of some of the failing traditions, you can take heart in the knowledge that all is not lost. It is not too late to develop your talent, which is the subject of this book. There is no age limit to creating music ability, and the steps to accomplishing this will be explained in the chapters that follow.

Please Visit: <u>www.talentcanbetaught.com</u>

Overcoming Failing Traditions with The Powerful PRAISE™ Techniques

"PRAISE" is an acronym for the six key elements that lead to success and which form the basis of The Talent CAN Be Taught System. Chapters 4 through 9 are devoted to presenting each of these six key elements for success in detail.

As a teacher and administrator, of course, I am always looking for ways to help both students and teachers to overcome the challenges resulting from the failing traditions. One of my most recent programs is a Teacher Apprentice program. The primary target group for this program is especially high school-age students in the Intermediate level grades of RCM piano instruction or higher. But I have also expanded it to include private teachers who have experienced the challenges of the failing traditions themselves and are seeking professional development in order to better serve their students. My goal has always been to provide this assistance to help teachers to grow rather than simply to look for other teachers. In past, I have even offered this assistance at no cost to my own teachers who are willing to embrace the principles, strategies, and terms of the Apprentice program to improve their approaches to music education.

Unfortunately, not all teachers are willing to upgrade their skills, even when this is offered to them at no financial cost, and even while they are still able to continue teaching. Sadly, many prefer instead to go elsewhere to teach where they can continue to use the same unsuccessful methods that they have always used...the methods described in the failing traditions.

Start well, and the finish will take care of itself!

For several years, now, I have been using this motto about starting well. Convinced that the first key to success is to start well, I began to implement strategies that eventually evolved into The Powerful PRAISE Techniques that now form the main components of The Talent CAN Be Taught System. And, these components are the keys to changing the failing traditions of Chapter 3. Each of the six key elements of PRAISE has two related parts. Understanding the six key elements necessarily begins in Chapter 4 with the single most important element of all; and that is Performance.

Part Two:

Creating Talent with

The Powerful PRAISE Techniques™

Chapter 4

Performance and Repertory:
The Core Essence of Music

The Powerful PRAISE™ Techniques

Performance & Repertory – The Core Essence of Music

Results & Accreditation – The Benchmarks of Achievement

Acceleration & Motivation – The MAGIC of Synergy™

Insights & Strategies – The Philosophy of Education

Supervision & Curriculum – The Tools of Instruction

Ear Training & Reading Skills – The Fundamentals of Learning

Performance

One might think that performance as a key skill to be developed by all musicians would be obvious, for without performance, there would be no music. Unlike the visual arts, music is a performance art. Yet it is the loss of this first skill that has led to so much frustration for so many students in their overall quest to develop their musical ability. Even more unfortunate is that the loss of this important skill also leads to the loss of *all* other music skills. As in so many things in life, the various elements of music are very interdependent. And, as with dominos, if the first one doesn't fall correctly, the entire chain is adversely affected, usually sooner, rather than later. A problem in one area usually leads to problems in other areas.

In short, there is a high level of interdependence among all of the keys for success, and it all starts with performance.

Music is a performance art;
if music is not performed, it doesn't exist

It is critical to understand any problem before we make any attempt to solve it. With that in mind, we might ask what problems exist with performance. Many factors might be blamed for what has been happening, such as societal attitudes, new technologies which might possibly undermine the interest that some may have in developing performance skills, or even the patience needed to make the effort. But I'm devoting these pages to consideration of challenges that can easily be overcome, and solutions that are within our power to almost immediately begin the process of achieving.

The Primary Deficiency Found in the Failing Traditions

I wrote in Chapter 3 that the signs of failing traditions have existed for many years, and that these traditions often involved students skipping grade levels of music study, and skipping parts of a curriculum of study which create serious gaps in learning. In addition, many students are studying as few as a dozen pieces over several years to get certificates which falsely indicate that they have actually developed certain music skills. And as if this isn't bad enough, some of these certified students then perpetuate or perhaps even escalate these failing traditions by teaching others.

All of the unfortunate circumstances that were detailed stem from one primary deficiency. And, that is that the teachers, parents, and students have placed no value whatsoever on performance. Pieces are only learned for an exam. Once the exam has been taken, the pieces are discarded like something that is no longer of any value. Books are returned to teachers, or sold, or given away. This attitude that devalues performance is at the heart of all that is wrong about many of the failing traditions in private music education.

Two Key Steps to Developing Performance Skills

So the first step to changing the failing traditions is the realization that creating music ability must begin first of all with a commitment to teach, and especially to model, the value of performance.

Performance should be encouraged from the very beginning

Performance is something that can begin with the very first piece of music that a student learns. The piece may consist of only one note repeated several times, and last just ten seconds, but performing it is the first important step to take.

Review should be a part of a student's everyday practice

As students learn ever more complex pieces of music, they should be encouraged to review pieces that they have already learned. This review should be a part of a student's everyday practice. In fact, in the early stages when a student doesn't know how to practice, and may even be too young to be taught how to practice, reviewing pieces that have already been learned should be the *only* thing that students are encouraged to do on their own.

As students progress through various levels, they may begin to review pieces from their previous books, to avoid forgetting music they've learned, grow their repertory, and continue to develop their reading skills. In total, before going for their very first RCM exam, even at a Preparatory A level, students should be able to perform more than one hundred short music selections either with the printed music, or by memory.

The Role of Memorization

Eventually, as students review pieces repeatedly, memorization will take place, and they may begin to play the pieces they know by memory. Memorizing pieces will become such a regular part of learning, that forfeiting marks on exams due to lack of memory will never be an issue. In addition, looking at the music page tends to be a distraction, and often hinders a successful performance particularly if the student is not totally focused on the page but sometimes looks down at the keyboard. Using the music can actually even cause a breakdown during performance that might not have otherwise happened.

So, performance is the first and most important key to student success, and it contributes to the development of many other music skills, as will be explained in the pages to come.

Three key steps to developing performance skills are:

1) Reviewing and performing the most recent pieces that are being learned while keeping eyes focused on the music notation on the page.

2) Reviewing and performing old pieces and old books of music that have already been learned while keeping eyes focused on the music notation on the page.

3) Reviewing and performing old pieces that have already been committed to memory, while keeping eyes focused on hands and keyboard.

Repertory

Hand in hand with performance is, of course, is having a repertory of pieces that can be performed. Without music to perform, performance cannot exist. In the beginning stages, emphasis on a particular style of music is not what is important. Developing performance skills is the key to performing the repertoire. Once developed, the skills can be applied to many varied styles. And, most good curricula will actually contain a variety of styles to ensure that the student is introduced to this at the earliest stage possible. A later chapter is devoted to the topic of curricula.

A personal repertory is a collection of music that one can perform anywhere, anytime, by memory. The evidence of learning is found in a person's ability to skillfully perform a large repertory of music

Building a repertory of music selections is accomplished through all of the same processes already outlined. Students acquire a repertory of pieces by performing, reviewing, and eventually memorizing the pieces they learn. In time, they may also begin to learn music by ear. This is also discussed in a later chapter.

A developing repertory of music should consist of three main collections of music:

1) Music from a curriculum or anthology for learning that is currently being studied.

2) Music from a curriculum or anthology learned previously in the near or distant past.

3) Music from other sources or music selections that may have been learned by ear.

I want to take time to point out that exposure to music on a regular basis at home, at school, and at church, has a significant role to play in the creating of music ability as well as for developing a large personal repertory of music. Further, the role of public education in providing this has diminished in recent years. One of the most important live music experiences that are available to most people is through a church community. Music is an integral part of worship in many faiths, and in particular, the Christian Church has a long and vibrant heritage of music which is easily accessible to families. My own music experience began with weekly if not even almost daily exposure to Christian music. Later on, this contributed to my ability to learn music, both from the printed page and by ear. From an early age, I began to learn to perform this music as well, and my ear was trained by listening to music and by having regular opportunities to sing, both at school and at church. By the time I reached high school, my music studies had expanded to include other instruments and a whole new and vast collection of music, in addition to which, as my skills continued to improve, I began to learn to play popular and other music by ear as well.

For students following in the failing traditions, tangible results in the form of music skills have in many cases been limited. And, even though many students may have been awarded certificates that do not accurately represent a solid foundation in their music skills because so many teachers and parents have chosen to diminish the system with shortcuts, there is still great value in accreditation. When used correctly, it is an important and valuable part of the process of creating musical ability, as we will discover in the next chapter.

Please visit: <ins>www.talentcanbetaught.com</ins>

Chapter 5

Results and Accreditation:
The Benchmarks of Achievement

The Powerful PRAISE Techniques™

Performance & Repertory – The Core Essence of Music

Results & Accreditation – The Benchmarks of Achievement

Acceleration & Motivation – The MAGIC of Synergy™

Insights & Strategies – The Philosophy of Education

Supervision & Curriculum – The Tools of Instruction

Ear Training & Reading Skills – The Fundamentals of Learning

Results

In Chapter 2, where I described some of the key signs of the failing tradition, I also noted that results, in the form of the development of music skills that may be used for life, had, by many people, been replaced with a goal to receive certificates simply for self-promotion, with minimal if any intent to ever use the actual music skills.

Despite the fact that many people have placed little value on results that relate to music education, or the actual development of music skills, tangible results in the form of music skill development, or growth, should be recognized as a very useful and admirable goal to achieve. In fact, developing these skills is the real purpose of having music lessons and the actual achievement that certificates are supposed to indicate. There are a great many music skills as well as proven procedures that may be used to measure these skills.

Three of the most useful music skills to develop include:

1   Ability to read music notation and accurately play at first sight what is written on the music page

2   Ability to listen to music, and immediately and accurately play what one hears

3   Ability to write in music notation the sounds that one hears by the ear or creates in the mind

Music Literacy and Performance

It is noteworthy that these basic music literacy skills, once again, begin and end with performance. The first two involve actually performing what is either seen (music notation) or heard (by listening). The third involves writing music notation to record what someone else is performing so that others will be able to read it and perform it. These re-affirm once again that performance is the core essence of music, and that without it, music would not exist, and music education would fail.

Other important music skills that relate to performing on the piano / keyboard:

1   Having an artistic touch on the keyboard to control articulations, dynamics, and phrasing

2   Developing the ability to use the pedals effectively to artistically enhance performance

3   Understanding and using stylistic elements that are essential to musical interpretation

These and other music-related skills should be the primary goal of having lessons. That is not to say that documenting success with certificates is not important, but just that it should not be the first priority. To make certification the priority is to put the proverbial cart before the horse. And as this old adage suggests, this lack of proper order creates a dysfunction which makes both the metaphorical cart and horse useless.

Accreditation

Once the goal of achieving practical music skills has been given its rightful place, it is important to recognize that accreditation has a valuable role to play in the learning process. Documents that honour achievement provide incentive for students to make further steps toward success. In addition, they also are a system of recording steps in the process of learning, or benchmarks for ongoing success.

Festival and exam reports, awards, and certificates honour achievements and provide benchmarks for ongoing success.

These awards and certificates only have merit, however, if they truly indicate the achievement of the music skills that they are intended to represent.

To Compete or Not to Compete

Many people downplay the value of music festivals, and make excuses for music students not rising to the challenge of using their skills to try to excel in a competitive setting. Some prefer a non-competitive approach where all are made to feel that their standards of performance are equally good. That is neither accurate, nor is it a very realistic view of life, however. In addition, such attitudes often do not motivate students to become better by lulling them into a sense of undeserved self-satisfaction.

There is, always has been, and always will be a competitive aspect to life in general. And, except in cases of nepotism, it is usually the best qualified, the most talented, and the most motivated and deserving who succeed. The challenge of competition, therefore, has a valuable role to play in motivating students to achieve the best possible results.

The Value and Limitations of Competition

One of the reasons that some educators do not value competition is that music and talent are things that are very subjective in nature. One person may value one particular skill, while another may place a higher priority on a different skill. And, of course, there are other factors that may impact the quality of a performance on any given day, so any competition or exam at best is only able to measure the performance of the moment and does not fully indicate the level of skill development that the performer has developed.

Still, the experience of the event, and the challenge that motivates students to excel is a valuable part of the learning process. And due recognition for a high quality of performance on a particular occasion, given to those who have earned it, more than compensates for the imperfections that are always a part of any music competition, or for that matter, any method of evaluation whatsoever in any other aspect of life.

Chapter 5 Summary

Growth of music skills, therefore, which are tangible and can be heard in performance, supported by documents such as awards and certificates, work together as an important aspect of the overall learning process.

For more information and free bonuses, please visit:

http://www.talentcanbetaught.com

Chapter 6

Acceleration and Motivation:
"The MAGIC of Synergy™"

The Powerful PRAISE Techniques™

Performance & Repertory – The Core Essence of Music

Results & Accreditation – The Benchmarks of Achievement

Acceleration & Motivation – The MAGIC of Synergy™

Insights & Strategies – The Philosophy of Education

Supervision & Curriculum – The Tools of Instruction

Ear Training & Reading Skills – The Fundamentals of Learning

Synergy

Synergy is the dynamic which takes place when two or more elements work together to achieve something that they would not otherwise achieve if used separately. And in choosing the six-letter word "PRAISE" to use as an acronym for presenting the six key elements, it was also with the knowledge that praise itself can be a very effective tool for helping to create a positive synergy for learning.

In music, the dynamic inter-connectivity of acceleration with motivation is a key factor. Perhaps one of the most sensational examples of synergy is the combination of nitric acid and glycerine, which, when combined create explosives such as dynamite. The synergy of these two elements in combination is so amazing, that the word "dynamite" has entered the language as a metaphoric expression referring to sensational power or success. Sometimes the words momentum or chemistry are also used to describe this phenomenon.

Synergy is also a very emotional factor in the process of creating talent. It has much to do with how we feel about our journey. A depressed or frustrated attitude cannot provide the positive energy that is needed for growth and success. Similarly, positive emotional experiences working together can create a powerful dynamic that fuels the learning experience. In fact, in his book, *The Talent Code*, Daniel Coyle also makes reference to musical experiences that give younger members of a family an advantage, and that are able to "fuel" success, as noted in Chapter Two.

Synergy is well known in sports as well as in the arts. In sports especially, synergy tends to be referred to as momentum in terms of a team, or possibly chemistry when describing compatibility of teammates. Hockey fans have all witnessed the transformation in performance that often occurs very suddenly when a team that was feeling defeated and performing as if there was no hope, suddenly gets a dose of adrenalin from an unexpected turn of events that energizes them beyond all rational explanation. And at the same time, the other team, that appeared to be totally in control just moments before, suddenly cannot seem to do the most basic things correctly, and are desperately trying to hang on to whatever advantage they currently have.

The Whole Can Be Greater Than the Sum of the Parts

On some occasions, members of a team seem to be able to perform together at a higher level than their respective skills would suggest. On paper, they might not seem to have enough talent, but when working together, each making a specific contribution in support of the common goal, they achieve far beyond expectations.

The story of the success of the Oakland Athletics baseball club is instructive. In 2002, the club had a much smaller budget than most of their adversaries, but manager Billy Beane assembled a team that together played at a much higher standard than was suggested by the records of its individual players. The A's amazing success was the subject of the movie *Moneyball*, starring Brad Pitt and based on Michael Lewis' 2003 book by the same name. It is a classic example of this synergy in action.

The MAGIC of Synergy

Synergy is important for success in just about everything in life, and developing music talent is no exception. Here, I have expanded the concept of the dynamic inter-connectivity of acceleration with motivation to include five important elements. The word "*MAGIC*" is an acronym for these elements which create synergy. These are not the only elements that create music ability synergistically, but they are five of the most important ones: Momentum, Acceleration, Growth, Inspiration, and Competition.

Momentum

It is a law of physics that things in motion tend to continue to move without a lot of effort, while things that are stationary take a considerable amount of effort just to get moving. So momentum is a very desirable element for success in music, as it is in sports. It has been said that "success breeds success,"   which is another way of explaining the same law of physics. As students recognize that their music skills are improving, they develop a sense of momentum and the desire to continue improving even more.   As previously stated, sometimes momentum begins to occur so dramatically and unexpectedly, that it is as if it happens magically, or perhaps, we might say "auto-magically," a term coined by author Raymond Aaron to describe a form of synergy which results in success appearing so effortlessly or seemingly automatically that it is as if it has occurred as a result of some supernatural power. And so, momentum is the first of the important elements that make up "The MAGIC of Synergy."

Acceleration

Acceleration is momentum on steroids. A slow speed of learning is one of the very important factors that lead to so many students giving up their quest to become musically talented.   While slow learning is the result of strategies and circumstances that have become a part of the "Failing Traditions," it is equally important to realize that accelerated learning has the effect of creating excitement and motivating students to even more actively continuing their quest for success. While momentum is simply the sense of moving forward or making progress, acceleration is a much higher and increasing rate of progress.

Learning quickly is an exciting experience, and well-developed reading skills are the single most important key to accelerated learning.

This is not a new concept, and I'm sure that as you are reading this, you can think of times in your own life when you were energized by the speed of learning which you experienced. When a student discovers that he or she can learn a piece of music in ten minutes rather than ten months, ten weeks, or even ten days, this has a powerful effect in motivating the student to continue working toward even more exciting goals. Accelerated learning naturally involves accumulating a growing performance repertory which was the topic of Chapter 3, and it is the second of the important elements that make up "The MAGIC of Synergy."

Growth

While learning quickly is important, the actual development of music skills is the ultimate goal, as already stated. So while acceleration has much to do with the fast development of a growing repertory of music, the growth which is referred to here is more closely associated with the actual music skills, such as those listed in Chapter 4 under the heading of "Results." Students must grow in their ability to perform skillfully, using their ever-increasing understanding of style, articulation, dynamics, phrasing, technic, and much more to create ever improving and more advanced levels and standards of performance. That is why growth, or results in terms of the development of music skills, is the third of the important elements that are keys to creating "The MAGIC of Synergy."

Inspiration

The word "inspiration" comes from Latin, and essentially it means "to breathe into." The word is often used in connection with spiritual experiences, or perhaps religious music, that might be said to be "God-breathed," and which, interestingly, fits a description that the composer Handel has attributed to his own composing of the famous and well-loved oratorio, *Messiah*. But it is also used quite frequently to describe the experience that people have when important ideas or insights come to them suddenly or even unexpectedly. Inspiration can result from listening to a great speaker, or discovering something of value that you had not previously considered. A great work of art, or a great performance can appear to be inspired, and certainly can also be very inspiring.

It is my hope that you will find this book inspiring, and that parents will be motivated to ensure that their children receive every ideal strategy for success with their private music lessons. It is my hope also that it will inspire those of you who previously experienced the failing traditions so that you may have a renewed hope and desire to develop the skills that you once set out to achieve.

Inspirational Teaching

And so, inspiration is also a valuable element in developing music skills for all music students. One of the ways that I try to inspire my own students is by demonstrating how to play the piece of music that they are learning. Sometimes I may also inspire students by performing other pieces that are much more challenging, perhaps even pieces that they have never heard before.   In both cases, what is at work is the realization by the student that there is a higher standard that can be achieved.

A Picture Is Worth Ten Thousand Words

As already mentioned, one of the failing traditions is that all too many teachers do not actually demonstrate for their students, despite the wisdom in the words of the Chinese philosopher Kung Fu Tzu (Confucius), that a picture is worth ten thousand words. *All* spoken description is inferior to *any* demonstration. Music, therefore, must be demonstrated to be fully understood.

And so, listening to, or even better, viewing well-performed pieces of great classical music can be very inspirational. In fact, I have often said that I learned more about music and was motivated to continue my pursuit of developing my music skills by listening to great music, more than from all of the lessons that I received from various teachers. By saying this, I don't intend any dis-respect to any of my teachers. To the contrary, I greatly appreciate the experiences I had with all of them, but the fact remains that the inspiration that I derived from listening to great music being performed was one of the most important aspects of my musical education.

Competition

Another very effective way of inspiring students is through competition, which is the next in the elements that create "The MAGIC of Synergy." The last letter in the acronym "MAGIC" is, of course, "C," which is for Competition.

A Competitive Instinct – A Tale of Two Girls

I have already discussed the value of competition and receiving awards for participation in music festivals in Chapter 4 under the topic of Accreditation. To reinforce its value further, however, I want to share an experience I had with one of my students. In June 2012, two of my students were progressing very well and both were also at about the same stage in their skill development and performing level. Both were taking the same level RCM exam that month. One student achieved 97% on the exam, which was our highest student mark in that particular exam session, while the other received only 87% at the same grade level, which happened also to be our lowest student mark in that exam session. Obviously, both deserved credit for outstanding achievement.

But what was particularly noteworthy, was what happened next. Both students moved forward to the next grade level and both scheduled an exam for August, just two months later. Both had developed the synergy that was needed to move up a grade in such a short time and still perform with excellence. By early July, however, I began to notice a difference in the student who had achieved just 87% in June. This girl was on a mission. Her level of intensity had dramatically increased. Everything she did was more focused. She had a personal goal that resulted from the realization that she was capable of doing just as well as the other student had the month before. The result was that despite the short time period involved, she was able to improve her mark to 93% on the next exam level in August, which happened to be the highest mark among all of our students in that exam session. And, yes, she also outperformed the other student the second time around. And so, competition is a very valuable element in creating "The MAGIC of Synergy."

Internal and External Competition

It should be noted also that competition can be both internal or personal, and external. It can be an internal motivation to equal or pass a previous personal standard of achievement, or to be recognized by others as successful. In other words, the source of the competition can be from a comparison with others or simply be an internal desire to get better. I think a little bit of both may have been at work in the above example of the student who improved her level of achievement in just two months.

Momentum, Acceleration, Growth, Inspiration, and Competition form The MAGIC of Synergy™ which has a valuable role to play in leading students to ever greater successes.

Confidence

Another "C" that I might have included, of course, is Confidence. And it goes virtually without saying that confidence is a very important element for success. In a sense, however, confidence is really just an outcome of The MAGIC of Synergy.

Confidence comes with success; and success comes with confidence.

Confidence develops naturally in conjunction with all of the other motivators which have been discussed here, growing at least proportionately if not even exponentially in relation to the overall success that the student experiences. Confidence comes with success, and success with confidence. And, the synergy of learning is the engine that drives it all.

Summary

The high degree of interconnectivity between Acceleration and Motivation are well established with The MAGIC of Synergy and so it stands as the third of The Powerful PRAISE Techniques. While The MAGIC of Synergy focuses on the role of emotion in creating talent, the next chapter has much more of a practical focus. It explores some of the philosophical principles relating to music education, along with a number of practical insights and strategies that are key to student success. These form the basis of the "10 Important Teaching Principles – Insights & Strategies for Learning."

For more information on The MAGIC of Synergy and inspirational stories of student successes, please visit www.talentcanbetaught.com

The Powerful PRAISE Techniques™

Performance & Repertory – The Core Essence of Music

Results & Accreditation – The Benchmarks of Achievement

Acceleration & Motivation – The MAGIC of Synergy™

Insights & Strategies – The Philosophy of Education

Supervision & Curriculum – The Tools of Instruction

Ear Training & Reading Skills – The Fundamentals of Learning

10 Important Teaching Principles

This chapter includes important tips, insights, and educational strategies that enable students to avoid the failing traditions. Many of these practical tips relate both to the process of independent practice, as well as to times when the teacher is present to provide expertise and direction.

Principle #1: Practice – A Double-Edged Sword!

While, as noted in the chapter on the failing traditions, all too many private teachers simply assign work for students. One of the most important principles of the Talent CAN Be Taught System is that independent practice is a double-edged sword that can sometimes create more problems than it is worth, particularly in the early stages of training. When the student is ready, strategies on how to practice can be taught, so that independent practice time can be used effectively, and so that emotional issues relating to slow progress or poor practice habits do not develop.

Knowing *how* to practice
is of much greater value
than knowing *what* to practice

In music, as in life, the most successful people are those who don't just work hard, but also "work smart."   For more mature and advanced students, therefore, having a plan for practice is an important strategy. It is smart, because practice time can be used more efficiently.

Principle #2: Remember – The Tortoise Beat the Hare!

A long-standing joke back in the days of vinyl recordings (in the 1950's and 60's, at a time when a three-speed player system included 33 1/3, 45, and 78 revolution per minute options on the record player) was of "cramming" for a listening test by playing a 33 1/3 speed recording at 78 rpms. While this may be a foreign language to most people today, the humour is related to the fact that anyone who ever tried to do that back in that era will have discovered that it causes the music to be played not only faster, but at a much higher pitch, making singers on the recording sound like Alvin and the Chipmunks.

Practicing quickly is the slowest way to learn

Notwithstanding the humour of the above situation, the reality, however, is that trying to practice quickly on a musical instrument winds up taking much longer than if discipline is exercised and the pace is slowed down as much as necessary in order to be able to practice without constant errors and hesitations. Everyone wants to learn fast, and the temptation, therefore, is to practice at a faster tempo. But, practicing quickly not only takes much longer, but often prevents a student from making the necessary corrections at all. Aesop's famous wisdom about the tortoise and the hare certainly applies here. So it is one of the greatest challenges for all private teachers to ensure that students play as slowly as is necessary in order to be able to play steadily until all hesitations and errors can be eliminated, and all the correct notes and rhythms are in their correct place. In some cases, the teacher must set the tempo for the student and ensure that the student maintains it while playing.

Principle #3: Repeating Mistakes – It's a Bad Decision!

Typically when practicing, students stop every time they make an error, correct it, and then continue. Sometimes students will even stop when no error has been made, and may repeat a note or two that was already played correctly just to buy time because they haven't figured out how to play what comes next. This is a sign that the student is trying to practice or learn a new piece at a tempo that is faster than they can manage. Flow and continuity never develops, and if the student does not slow down, the same errors, hesitations, and corrections tend to re-occur every time.

**Making mistakes is a part of practicing
just as it is a part of everyday life;
but repeating the mistakes is just a bad decision
that simply requires a better practice plan.**

As part of a practice routine, therefore, it is important to teach students to pause, assess what went wrong, and then repeat the passage for the purpose of correcting at the very least one error each time.

Principle #4: Practice – It Doesn't Make Perfect!

Sometimes when practicing, as has been mentioned, a student will make an error, stop, make the correction and then continue. This often happens if the student is practicing more quickly than their brain can digest the information on the music page, as was noted in #2 above. In effect, then, they are repeatedly practicing the very errors, hesitations, and corrections that they want to eliminate, rather than learning to avoid the hesitations and play the passage correctly.

Therefore, by stopping to correct an original error such as a wrong note, the student has actually made a second error...that of stopping. And this is a rhythmic error, which is a greater problem than a wrong note. This is sometimes followed by repeating the passage with almost identical results.

Now, the student has actually practiced the error, the stop, and the correction, perfecting the repetition of the error; instead of pausing, thinking about what to correct, and then doing it correctly.

Practice does not make perfect;
only perfect practice makes perfect
– Vince Lombardi

Unfortunately, students sometimes get into a habit of duplicating the same errors, hesitations, and corrections every time they play. The result is imperfect practice, which is not simply imperfect, but even worse, is actually practicing making errors and hesitations, which means that the student is perfecting the process of performing errors. Practicing in this way never leads to perfection, and these learned errors become even more difficult to correct later on.

Hesitations that are practiced and become habits also prevent students from ever increasing the tempo or speed, because doing so aggravates the situation by increasing the number of errors and hesitations as well as the level of frustration experienced by the student. All errors and hesitations must first be eliminated while still practicing at a slow tempo, before increasing the tempo can be successful.

Principle #5: Performing – It Isn't About Correct Notes!

The quality of a performance is not found in the number or percentage of correct notes that are played, but rather in the overall effect of the performance. And as mentioned, rhythm, not the actual notes, is the more vital ingredient. It is absolutely essential that students learn the correct rhythm at the time that they are learning the notes, if the rhythm has not actually been learned first with strategies such as clapping and counting. That will help to alleviate the frustration that results from repeating errors and hesitations.

Playing with rhythmic accuracy can lead to a successful performance despite a multitude of wrong notes; but playing all of the right notes with rhythmic errors is just a poor performance

Rhythm is what gives music notes and pieces of music their distinctive character or identity. Without the correct rhythm, the music is simply wrong. However if the rhythm is correct, a performance can still be effective despite the presence of wrong notes. The power of rhythm in creating a great performance is illustrated very effectively in the following performance that I recently heard at a local music festival:

A Lesson at a Local Music Festival

A talented student was playing in a Grade 6 RCM Sonatina and Sonata class. It was unfortunate that the only flaws in her entire performance came during the final four bars of the piece, during which she made note errors in her left hand seemingly on almost every beat of the final four bars. Throughout these final four bars which concluded the movement, however, she was able to maintain the accuracy of her right hand, as well as the rhythm, the dynamics, and the stylistic touch and articulations which embodied the real character of the piece. And, most important of all, she never once hesitated or stopped playing to make a correction. I'm sure she was disappointed with the way she finished the selection, but she still managed to maintain the integrity of the music. She also displayed an air of professionalism, graciously acknowledging the applause, and smiling as she took her bow before returning to her seat. She sat down in the row in front of me, and seeing that she felt bad about what had happened, I leaned forward to offer her a word of encouragement. I whispered "Congratulations...you performed very well...you made it sound right." As it happened, the adjudicator awarded her first place in the category, which she certainly had earned. Afterward, I asked her, somewhat rhetorically, "Are you surprised that you won the first award?" Not really expecting an answer, I then congratulated her yet again saying, "Remember, it's all about the performance. You didn't stop because of the errors, and yours was the best performance, so the note errors really didn't matter. Always remember that."

Principle #6: Practicing – It Starts on the Second Attempt!

Playing through a new piece of music from beginning to end can be a very tedious process, especially if there are numerous errors and hesitations along the way. Yet this is what many students consider to be practicing. The reality is that even when the student reaches the end of the piece, practice still has not even begun, because it is not until a passage is attempted a second time that it is even possible to begin true practicing by working to correct errors that may have occurred the first time.

Practice doesn't even begin until the second attempt!

And so, not only is playing a piece all the way through very unproductive and time-consuming, but it does not even qualify as practice at all. A far better strategy is to focus the same length of time on just a very few bars of music and repeat them frequently to develop both fluency and accuracy. In short, practice does not begin until the second attempt

Principle #7: Learning to Play fast – It can be easy!

Increasing the tempo (or speed) of a piece of music that has first been practiced slowly, steadily, and accurately, is a very easy part of the learning process, and it also takes the least amount of time.

Previously, I noted that practicing quickly is the slowest way to learn. But once the notes and rhythm of a new piece of music have been learned correctly, the process of gradually increasing the speed can be accomplished quickly and easily, often in a matter of minutes. A metronome is a very useful tool for achieving this because the speed can be increased by increments that are very small and almost imperceptible. And so, increasing the tempo of something that has already been learned accurately at a slow speed can actually be quite easy. But attempting to practice quickly without first ensuring the accuracy of both rhythm and note leads both to the practicing of errors and hesitations which prevent the student from ever developing fluency and style.

Principle #8: Eye Focus – On the Page or On the Keyboard?

When learning to type on a computer keyboard, looking at the screen causes the typist to lose their place in the document being copied. In the same way, a student learning a new piece must not allow focus to wander away from the music page. Looking away and then looking back at the music page often leads to confusion, playing errors, and even hesitations, all caused from re-focusing on the wrong place in the music, or attempting to find the correct spot. This can easily be avoided simply by not taking eyes off the music page.

When reading and learning music, eyes should be kept on the music page; if performing music by memory, eyes may then focus on the hands and keyboard

Keeping eyes on the notes on the music page is sometimes challenging to do if the piece tends to involve big leaps for the hands, in which case, of course, the best solution is for the performer to memorize the music so that focus can be directed entirely toward the hands on the keyboard.

Principle #9: The #1 Worst Learning Strategy – EVER!

Writing letter names under notes on the page is generally a very bad strategy, and as one that has helped to create the "Failing Traditions" it is usually best to avoid it altogether. The reason that it is problematic is that it teaches the student not to focus on the real music notation. The assumption is that finding the notes is the most important part, which simply is not true, and leads to another of the failing traditions (not making rhythm the first priority).

In addition the reason writing letter names under notes has become necessary in the first place is because the students are often attempting to learn music without having developed basic novice level notation reading skills, which is yet another of these failing traditions.

Finally, by following only letter names, all of the other information that the music notation contains is missed altogether, including which register, duration, articulation, accidentals, hand, fingering, phrasing, and more are to be employed. Simply put, not only is it an enormous distraction for the learner, but it actually undermines reading skill development.

Writing letter names under notes is a strategy that has merit only as a limited exercise at the Primer or Novice level, or for beginning theory studies.

Music notation is a language that must be learned, and nobody can learn a foreign language in the first place by being allowed to focus only on a translation of the original words. And at best, letter names written under notes represent only a very partial translation of the information in the notation symbols, making the entire process of absolutely no value whatsoever beyond the Primer or Novice level. Students unable to read music notation should make addressing this challenge their first priority.

Principle #10: Work Backwards – A Useful Strategy!

Traditionally, students usually start at the beginning of a piece of music and work through toward the end. That is why the best-performed part of the piece is usually right at the beginning, because that is the part that tends to get the most practice. After that, the process tends to become slower and filled with more and more errors until it grinds to a halt, after which the student often returns to the beginning. This method of practicing means that the piece gets gradually worse with each passing bar, and this can be a very frustrating way to practice, very uninspiring to the learner, and one that fails to motivate the student to continue.

Working backwards through a piece of music can actually be a more effective and motivational approach than starting at the beginning.

Working from the end, however, starting with the last few bars and gradually backing up through the piece has the opposite result, ensuring that the most unfamiliar and least well-played part is right at the start of each attempt, and the piece continues to improve bar by bar as familiarity with previously practiced bars of music increases all the way to the end. Psychologically, it is a much more pleasing experience to feel like the piece is getting progressively better rather than progressively worse, and the student is motivated to continue practicing as a result.

The analogy that fits this process of gradually backing up through a piece of music in order to move forward during the learning stages is somewhat similar to the process a starting pitcher goes through in the bullpen prior to the start of a baseball game. The pitcher doesn't start throwing from the bullpen mound, but rather makes a shorter, softer toss to the catcher from somewhere in front of the mound, and then after each pitch takes a step back, gradually making a longer and stronger throw until reaching the top of the bullpen mound.

The Achievers Programs™

An Additional Special Insight and Strategy

A minimum of 90-minutes per week of private lessons is a proven strategy that allows for development of the all-important synergy of learning on which students are able to thrive. This has been an important key to the success of the Achievers Programs™.

The value of this important scheduling strategy will be discussed in detail in Chapter 9.

For more insights on strategies for learning, please visit: www.talentcanbetaught.com

Chapter 8

Supervision and Curriculum:
The Tools of Instruction

The Powerful PRAISE Techniques™

Performance & Repertory – The Core Essence of Music

Results & Accreditation – The Benchmarks of Achievement

Acceleration & Motivation – The MAGIC of Synergy™

Insights & Strategies – The Philosophy of Education

Supervision & Curriculum – The Tools of Instruction

Ear Training & Reading Skills – The Fundamentals of Learning

Supervision & Curriculum

There is an aspect of supervision and curriculum that is applicable both to students and to their teachers.

Regular expert guidance closely following the curriculum resources ensures that all concepts are both taught and learned

Supervision

The high quality of Finnish education depends on the high quality of Finnish teachers."
– Pekka Himanen
(From: *The Talent Code* by Daniel Coyle)

Most people recognize the value of teachers, and the obvious and important connection between teaching and learning. This is especially evident in some of the causes of the failing traditions discussed in Chapter 3. A critical part of the process, however, of both teaching and learning is that both teachers and students require supervision. A student needs the expert guidance of the teacher. And the teachers need not only training and experience, but mentorship and/or professional development in order to ensure that they continue to improve and provide the best guidance possible for their students. Many independent private teachers do not plan for personal professional development experiences, nor do many have any interest in upgrading either their skills or their methods of teaching.

For the student, regular expert guidance closely following the curriculum resources ensures that all concepts are learned.

Teacher direction, rather than independent practice, is a more important key to learning for the student. Working independently can be a dangerous thing for a beginning student to have to do, unless the independent work is limited to review of things already learned.

For the teacher, regular support, supervision, and opportunity for personal growth ensures that all concepts are taught well.

Without supervision and professional development, all teachers are destined to re-create their own weaknesses in their students.

Curriculum

An excellent curriculum can go a long way to overcoming teacher weaknesses if it is used in a dedicated manner...skipping no pages in books of the curriculum...no books in each level of the curriculum...and no levels in the curriculum itself. However, the evidence of the failing traditions reveal that curriculum materials are being skipped regularly in all three of the ways listed above, by students of independent private teachers for reasons already outlined in chapter 1.

Both teachers and students require a curriculum to follow for two main reasons:

1. Not following a curriculum will result in the tendency to skip content and even grade levels, which causes great gaps in learning. Even great teachers will inadvertently neglect certain concepts if they are not following a comprehensive and sequential curriculum.

2. Typically, private music teachers only address teaching points that happen to appear in a particular piece of music. If music selection is random, or limited, as is the case more often than not, so is the instruction.

The primary tool for learning must be an outstanding curriculum that is both comprehensive and logically sequential.

One of the hallmarks of Talent CAN Be Taught is the exclusive use of what, in my opinion, is the best available piano curriculum on the market today. That is why we have made it our studio's house curriculum. It is the Piano Adventures curriculum by Nancy and Randall Faber. All TCBT teachers are expected to use this curriculum in its entirety. No part of it may be skipped so that no teaching concepts are missed.

A House Curriculum
Piano Adventures by Nancy & Randall Faber

There are four core books of this curriculum:

Lessons
Technique & Artistry
Theory
Performance

For those interested in other instrumental or vocal studies, it should be noted that piano keyboard instruction serves as a very valuable foundation for all music studies. This is so important, in fact, that some of the best private vocal teachers that I know insist that their vocal students also study piano.

For those who want to follow the RCM curriculum and receive accreditation, it must be kept in mind that RCM books are not a curriculum. Rather, they are simply carefully graded collections or anthologies of music and other materials. They are an excellent resource, but require a teacher to either plan a curriculum or course of study or use a published one such as Piano Adventures in conjunction with these RCM materials in order to ensure that they teach everything that a student needs to know.

Each of the four core books has a specific function in the training of students, which is why skipping some of the books always has serious consequences. The Lessons book contains all of the teaching concepts that the student needs to learn, starting from the very beginning and continuing over several levels up to the equivalent of about Grade 3 or 4 RCM. The Technique and Artistry book is all about learning how to play with style through developing technical skills. The Theory book contains written exercises to reinforce concepts that students are learning such as basic ear training and reading skills. And the Performance book is a very useful diagnostic tool for the teacher if used after completion of the Lesson book, as it helps to confirm how well reading skills are developing. There are also a number of support materials such as flash cards for symbol recognition and supplemental pieces if students have a particular interest in music selections such as Broadway show tunes or popular songs.

The four core books of the Piano Adventures curriculum serve as a daybook for the teacher. Closely following a comprehensive and sequential curriculum allows a teacher to track student progress by covering every page and explaining the teaching concepts to the students as they appear, thereby ensuring that no part of the curriculum is neglected. Without either a good curriculum of study that is strictly and completely followed, or a very carefully prepared daybook that includes a plan for teaching all music concepts, even the very best of teachers will be unable to ensure that students do not develop gaps in their learning which will eventually become liabilities.

At the appropriate level, students should be encouraged to use RCM materials as well, however, we insist that this still must be done in conjunction with a continuation of the basic curriculum. This is important because, simply making selections from these RCM anthologies, which is one of the most common liabilities of the failing traditions, does not ensure that all the necessary music concepts are taught.

One further note: I have been using the adjectives "sequential" and "comprehensive" in describing necessities for a curriculum of studies. This is because not all curricula combine these important attributes. In fact, I personally have been very puzzled by some method books which seem to have significant changes in the degree of difficulty and learning concepts even in consecutive selections when moving from one page to the next. This may account in part for the tendency of many independent private teachers to skip pages of some curriculum books. It can be very frustrating for a student to be learning one simple concept and then immediately be thrust into what seems to be an unreasonably difficult one on the very next page without the opportunity to develop a bit of a comfort level. And, I have never yet met a student coming from a previous teacher who used one of these other method books who did not say that some pages had been skipped. Invariably, these students also have difficulty remembering exactly which pieces they learned and have forgotten, as opposed to those that were just skipped altogether.

The end result of a curriculum that is not designed well from a sequential perspective, even if followed completely, is that it will stall the development of the synergy of learning that is so important to success, and which was the subject of Chapter 6. And, of course, it goes without saying that if the curriculum is not comprehensive, then learning gaps will also develop.

The last of The Powerful PRAISE Techniques and perhaps the most neglected aspect of music training, *Ear Training and Reading Skills*, is the focus of the next chapter.

For more information on courses of study with the Talent CAN Be Taught system, please visit:

www.talentcanbetaught.com

Chapter 9

Ear Training and Reading Skills:
The Fundamentals of Learning

The Powerful PRAISE Techniques™

Performance & Repertory – The Core Essence of Music

Results & Accreditation – The Benchmarks of Achievement

Acceleration & Motivation – The MAGIC of Synergy™

Insights & Strategies – The Philosophy of Education

Supervision & Curriculum – The Tools of Instruction

Ear Training & Reading Skills – The Fundamentals of Learning

When I was growing up, people who took an interest in my musical development and who saw me playing by memory often asked whether I read music, or played by ear. The answer, of course, particularly during my latter years of study was always "both." But the question itself is insightful, because it sums up the two most important of all music skills; the ability to play by sight, by reading the notation on the printed page, and the ability to play by ear, by hearing and comprehending the sounds, and translating them into the fingers.

These two supremely important and fundamentally basic of all music skills, surprisingly, are also the two most severely neglected and underdeveloped of all skills, mainly because of the strategies used by teachers and students who are participants in the failing traditions. As indicated previously, many students who manage to pass RCM exams and acquire a certificate, often do so in spite of receiving very low marks in these two vitally important areas of testing.

Ear Training

Ear Training enables students to both write and perform music that they hear, which is the intended outcome of developing a musical ear.

Ear training is a process which develops over a number of years. The two most important factors for developing a musical ear are also two of the most neglected of all learning strategies...listening to music, and singing.

Listening to Music

The first very important strategy for developing a musical ear is to simply listen to great music on a regular basis. Yet this is something that many students never do, and even the more serious and advanced students do only when required as part of their preparation for the RCM History exams.

I was told by my parents that I began listening to the Metropolitan Opera radio broadcast on Saturday afternoons at the age of four. Apparently, I was intrigued by the sounds on the radio, as well perhaps by the radio dial itself. A four-year old, of course, isn't sophisticated enough to know that listening to opera isn't considered cool by many people. So, inadvertently, with no pre-conceived notions, nor any specific intent, I was actually training my own ear by listening to great music. It was by chance that I just happened to use a very successful strategy for training the ear. Listening to great music or being surrounded by a musical environment provides, as previously mentioned, what Daniel Coyle, author of *The Talent Code*, describes as "fuel."

Why Classical Music?

Undoubtedly, someone will take exception to my suggestion that listening to great classical music is necessary. They may perhaps even suggest that any and all music should be able to accomplish the same thing. So I want to take time briefly to explain why classical music is the key; and likewise, to explain why much of popular music has limitations. The key lies in understanding the elements or ingredients of so-called "classical" music.

What are the Elements of Music?

While my intent is not to give a treatise on the fundamental elements of music, in order to satisfactorily explain why listening to classical music is the key, I do need to start with a brief explanation. So, here are fourteen of the main music elements along with a brief working definition for each:

---

14 Important Elements of Music

Rhythm – a series of sounds of varying durations that create an artistic pattern

Metre – division of the music into small segments or measures marked by strong and weak beats

Melody – a series of sounds of different pitches, rising and falling to create a tune

Harmony – a combination of two or more different pitches that sound pleasing together

Tempo – the pace or speed of a piece of music

Dynamics – the volume of sound, and variation between loud and quiet sounds

Phrasing – shaping segments of the music, moving toward or away from climactic points

Articulations – touch or starting attack of sounds and force with which they are played

Colour – different sounds or tones created by various instruments and voices

Texture – richness created by different voices, instruments, or parts working together

Form – organization of musical ideas or structure created either by repetition or variation

Balance – combining sounds that work together while maintaining their unique colours

Blend – combining sounds in ways that create a homogeneous melting pot effect

Style – the ways all elements are used by musicians in different eras and places in history

So, Why Not Listen to Popular Music?

I am not saying not to listen to popular music, however, making decisions about listening choices that have the greatest educational value will save a lot of time for the student. Listening to any kind of music can be fun, but the educational value of some may be limiting for very important reasons. Eating chocolate ice cream is enjoyable, but it's not a food group.

Characteristics That Limit the Educational Value of Popular Music for Ear Training

A typical piece of popular music may contain the following elements:

- Usually, a single repeated rhythmic idea or fragment

- Usually, a single metre, most frequently common time (4/4)

- Sometimes, a very limited melody with few notes in repetition, in a small range

- Very limited harmonic ideas, sometimes as few as two or three

- Usually just a single tempo throughout the selection

- Usually just a single volume level throughout the selection

- Phrasing may be repetitive or impeded by the limited range of melodies

- Few if any variations in instrumental articulations, as focus is usually on vocals.

- Often a single colour due to a particular mix of sounds, instruments, and voices

- Limited textures, which like colours, usually create a single style of sound

- The form is often in only two main parts, perhaps identified as a verse & refrain

- Balance or blend choices may over-emphasize one element at expense of others

- Pre-determined style creates devotees of one while not exploring other options

Summary of Popular Music Characteristics

So, in summary, regardless of the type of popular music, the consistent characteristic of popular music can be described as simplicity or perhaps even singularity in the use of musical elements. By using only one or very few options for each of the elements of music, or perhaps due to the minimizing if not eliminating of some musical elements altogether, popular music is less able to awaken the listener to the infinite number of variations or subtleties that are available or that are able to enhance a musical selection. In other words, within a single piece of popular music, there are few, if any degrees or variations of shadings in the way that virtually all of the elements are used.

Now, of course, it is true that comparing different popular selections may reveal use of a different tempo, or different metre, or different instruments, or different volume level, and so on. But understanding that all or most of the elements can be varied constantly, and experiencing the excitement and power associated with such an inexhaustible collection or palate of musical ideas is exclusively the domain of so-called "art music" or "classical" music.

It is also true that many well-trained, classically trained, or musically intuitive popular musicians of both the past and present such as the Beatles, Chicago, Elton John, Billy Joel, Linda Ronstadt, Diana Krall, and countless more have established a niche for themselves by paying more detail to some of the possible subtleties of musical expression. But the main characteristic of most popular music is simplicity, if not even uniformity. In addition, when some popular artists establish a niche or reputation for excellence, it is usually by employing the subtleties of musical expression that are usually the hallmark of classical music.

In fact, their interpretive style or approach in these cases may actually be referred to as a classical treatment. In short, what they are really doing is simply using more of the tools of the trade, rather than reducing their art to its most basic level.

In effect, to make another food analogy, trying to learn about musical elements by listening to popular music would be like trying to understand culinary arts by sampling peanut butter sandwiches. Or, perhaps, it might be compared to trying to learn about the various components of a balanced diet by studying the food groups involved in a meal comprised of pasta, rice, French fries and garlic toast.

In other words, listening to great classical music is important because it trains the ear using the full range of musical options.

What about Recent Trends in Popular Music?

In recent years, there has been a trend toward even greater simplification of popular music. One of the elements of music that has suffered the most from this trend toward simplification is melody. Many melodies of recent songs do not build toward or away from any climactic point at all. In fact, many songs, as just mentioned, consist of just a couple or very few notes which, rather than being phrased to give them a particular shape or direction, are instead just used in a basic alternating or repeated pattern which drastically limits the shape of the musical line and overall musical artistry. In these cases the performer relies on using other elements such as rhythm, or tone colour, or perhaps the lyrics to create the interest. Another interesting by-product of this trend is that because of the lack of melodic shape in some popular styles today, listeners are seldom motivated to sing along, but may, however, only chant or tap along with the rhythm and words if these inspire them to do so. And so, a diminishing interest in singing, which is the second important key to developing a musical ear, is also a casualty of the most recent pop music limitations.

Having acknowledged the recent decline of melody in general in much of popular music, (with some melodies, as noted, consisting of as few as one or two notes throughout long stretches of the song, or even, as in some cases such as rap music having no melodic line at all), it should also be noted that a number of young artists are turning the clock back. The style of the crooners of many years ago, such as Frank Sinatra and

Tony Bennett, and an era when melody was used much more significantly is enjoying a revival. Some recent popular artists, such as Michael Buble, are able to find a niche in contemporary popular music simply because of the fact that they utilize melody to a much greater extent. This, in turn, provides a bit of an oasis, at least from a melodic perspective, in an otherwise desert-like musical landscape.

A Parallel in Police Work

A great example of the impact of such limitations in another setting is found in police work. An interesting study that was reported a number of years ago, is that when witnesses of Asian heritage were asked to give a description of a suspect to police, their focus was not on hair colour. They may have noticed height, or clothing, or other characteristics in much more detail than people of other heritage, but because most people of their own culture usually had black hair, they simply had never learned to focus on it as a distinguishing characteristic, and so often were unable to identify it. If this is changing today, it is likely because of the exposure over a long period of time to more variance of hair colour than what they previously experienced in their own culture. Once again, therefore, the key to even considering the possibility of options is to have the opportunity to first experience them.

Another example that relates to police detective work involves getting witness accounts of traffic accidents. Depending especially on their vantage point, witnesses in different locations at the same intersection may have very different and even seemingly contradictory perspectives on the sequence of events. In fact, someone with an aerial view of the situation might have a better perspective than any of the witnesses at ground level.

For the very same reason, sports teams often have someone positioned in a box seat high in the arena or stadium to report what they see to the coach on the ground or at ice level. Likewise, those closest to a challenge sometimes are unable to see potential solutions as well as those who have a "birds-eye view" perspective.

In the same way, classical music, with all of its intricacies and full, limitless range of artistic possibilities must be experienced in order to provide the best possible method of ear training through listening.

Vocal Experience

As mentioned, the second but also very important strategy for ear training involves singing. It is possible to play an instrument such as the clarinet or piano and even play the correct notes without really listening to what you are playing. A violinist, however, actually has to be able to listen and adjust finger position constantly in accordance with what they hear in order to play in tune. Novice pianists or clarinetists may have no idea what sound to expect when they get ready to play a particular note. For the most part, if they play the right key, they get the right note, even though they may actually be surprised by the sound that they get when they play it. But, due to the nature of the instrument, trumpet players may actually play the wrong note even when using the correct valve combination or fingering if they do not first prepare themselves to play by hearing in their mind the sound of the note that they intend to play.

In the same way, singing correct notes involves a special effort to actually have the sounds in mind first, and to listen to the sounds while singing, which is similar to playing the violin or a brass instrument. As a result, even for experienced musicians, it is more challenging to have to sing the notes on the page rather than simply play them on the piano, because of the need to first hear the sound in their head before attempting to sing it. So singing is a great strategy to develop a musical ear.

It is noteworthy that all of the very best instrumentalists can also sing. A great symphony orchestra would sound like a choir if they were to put down their instruments and sing together. In fact, nobody becomes a truly great instrumentalist without being able to sing. That is not to say that they have great voices, but rather that they have developed a musical ear, and so have the ability to sing in tune as well as to listen and blend with other singers.

Most actors and actresses can also sing, even though most probably would not consider themselves to be singers. And, for some, you might think that the very idea of singing would appear to be contrary to the persona that they have as actors. The idea of Jack Nicholson singing an old sentimental French love song called "La vie en rose," for example is not exactly in keeping with the characters that he has played in many of his earlier Hollywood films or the persona or image that he often portrays. But, in fact, you can check him out online, singing this very song. Simply type in his name and the title in a search engine, and be prepared to be surprised. Or use the following link:

http://www.youtube.com/watch?v=ZZ9uijGlp2c

One of the easiest ways to get some singing experience is in a school choir or at church. Singing should also be a part of the everyday instrumental music learning experience for all students. In particular, beginning piano students should sing the notes as they play. This will help with both developing reading skills and ear training.

There are three ways of playing and singing together as a learning strategy especially at the novice level:

- Play and sing the note names – C, D, E, F, etc.

- Play and sing the beat numbers and play the notes – 1, 2, 3, 4, etc.

- Play and sing the words that are usually included in beginning piano books

Summary of Ear Training

The two most important keys that help to develop a musical ear are:

- Listening to great classical music on a regular basis

- Singing at every opportunity, both individually, and with others, especially throughout the years of training

Reading Skills

The ability to read music is not only the single most important factor for long-term success, but the one that specifically contributes most directly to accelerated learning.

Reading skill development should start at the very beginning, when both the notes and rhythm are very basic. There are two especially good ways that can be done in the early stages of studying piano:

- Clap (the rhythm) and count (the beats) before trying to play the notes

- Play the notes (with the correct rhythm) and count the beats while playing after the first step of clapping and counting has been done successfully

The Role of Review in Developing Reading Skills

Continual review is a very important strategy, for memorization, developing fluency, building a repertory, and, most importantly in the context of this chapter, improving reading skills. Review of pieces already learned should be a regular part of every practice every day. Again, in the early stages, before students have been taught how to practice, review of pieces already learned should be the only practice that students are asked to do on their own. By the time a student goes for their very first RCM exam (possibly a Preparatory A exam for piano) they should be able to play over 100 short pieces, including many from memory.

These strategies also help students to develop the MAGIC of Synergy, develop greater comfort with technical requirements, and become better sight readers. Rather than wondering if they will do well enough to pass the exam, the only question on their mind is how close to perfection they can achieve. At each new level of study, the student has an ever-increasing number of music selections that they have already learned, and that form a part of their repertory for ongoing review. They always have pieces that they can perform on a moment's notice, by memory.

This entirely different mindset relating to performance and the high degree of self-esteem that go with it also contribute to ongoing success.

Summary of Reading Skill Development

As students progress through the various levels of instruction, they should be encouraged to learn additional supplemental pieces that are neither in their main curriculum of study nor the RCM anthologies or collections of music. And, as they develop a musical ear, they should be encouraged to try playing pieces that they've heard, and for which they don't have printed music.

Those students who begin to show a very special talent in terms of a fast-growing ability to play by ear and read music by sight may also be offered more advanced challenges to supplement their learning and receive special recognition, without sacrificing any of the basic steps in the process.

The Fundamentals of Learning of Reading Skills and Ear Training are the last of The Powerful PRAISE Techniques. One of the most important of all strategies, and the one that is at the heart of creating talent in students, is our next focus. This next strategy, which is the foundation of the Achievers Programs, is the subject of Chapter 10.

Please visit: <u>www.talentcanbetaught.com</u>

Part Three:

Implementing a Winning System

Chapter 10

The Achievers Programs™

The greatest discovery of my generation
is that human beings can alter their lives
by altering their attitude of mind
— William James, Psychologist

The idea of creating The Talent Can Be Taught System had been in my mind for some time. The catalyst for starting it as a pilot program came in March 2010, when a mother told me of her intention to discontinue guitar lessons for her son after a trial month of four half-hour lessons because he had not been faithful in practicing for the last two weeks of the month. While I knew that my strategy would work for him, I had not been prepared for the sensational results that were to follow.

Following the student's last guitar lesson in his four-week trial month, I recommended that we try a different approach with him which had five main criteria. This served as a pilot program before I formally introduced the system as an option for all of our students.

Strategies for the Pilot Program

- Switch to piano lessons where an outstanding curriculum would help ensure success

- Schedule three half-hour lessons per week instead of one

- Provide a discount on the per-lesson rate to help compensate for the added expense

- Make a deal with the student that he didn't have to practice

- Qualify the practice arrangement by saying that if he insisted on practicing, that it should be no more than five minutes a day, and only on pieces that he had already been taught in a lesson

There were a number of important principles at work in my mind and objectives that I wanted to accomplish when I created this program. The following were my main objectives:

- to make practice issues irrelevant due to more frequent, regular teacher support

- to create synergy among the various learning components also with the frequency of instruction

- to reduce per lesson cost to encourage parents to make the larger overall financial commitment

- to ensure that the curriculum and course of study (on piano) would enhance student learning

- to eliminate the source of tension that had developed over independent home practice routines

At the beginning of June, less than three months later, as the student was asking his mother to purchase the fifth level books in the piano curriculum series, and I was questioning him to see if he was ready for it, his mother gave me this account of what had transpired after we changed the plan and adopted the five strategies for the pilot program listed above:

Oh, I forgot to tell you. He won't stop practicing. He practices at all hours during the day, even first thing in the morning before school. I put an alarm clock on the piano set for 8:15 AM. I tell him that when the alarm goes off, he has to stop playing the piano and go to school, or he is going to be late. I may be upstairs vacuuming and hear the alarm go off. I turn off the vacuum cleaner to listen, and the sounds from the piano keep on going. So I have to come downstairs to physically remove him from the piano and send him off to school.

So what happened here?

1. The student no longer had to practice. He wanted to practice, so he wasn't developing any pressure-related attitude issues.

2. He was getting frequent teacher direction using a great and thorough curriculum, so he was not falling into bad habits.

3. He was studying an instrument that provides a solid foundation for music skill development.

4. His success was creating a synergy or level of excitement that motivated him.

5. And, due to the lesson frequency (three half-hours per week), he learned more in less than three months than most students learn in three years, thereby achieving great success at a much lower cost to his parents.

Modifications to the Achievers Programs™

As time passed, I also addressed special needs by making revisions to meet the following goals:

- to offer group instruction as a FREE value-added bonus to assist in developing basic skills

- to promote and guarantee First Class Honours achievement on RCM exams as my responsibility

- to implement strategies for monitoring student learning and teacher direction

- to ensure that all students and teachers followed the studio's curriculum

- to encourage parents to "start well" by beginning with piano/keyboard instruction

A minimum of 1.5 hours per week of private lessons is a proven strategy that helps students to enjoy the all-important synergy of learning on which skill development is able to thrive.

Each of the principles around which the program was created, sought to accomplish the goals which eventually evolved into *The Powerful PRAISE Techniques* that have been explained in the previous chapters.

Reasons for focusing on each of these principles:

- Practice is a double-edged sword that often causes as much harm as it does good. Students who have not been taught how to practice, or may even be too young to be expected to be able to practice efficiently, will likely not benefit much from practicing independently. In addition, practice issues often become the lightning rod that leads to giving up.

- More frequent professional support from qualified teachers is a better alternative to practice, especially in the early stages, as well as for eliminating a need to review during lessons what has previously been taught but forgotten in the interim (usually seven days). More frequent lessons also helps eliminate errors learned during independent practice time that would need to be corrected.

- The frequency of lessons (including recommendation of a minimum of three half-hour private lessons per week) was also the key to developing what I later referred to as "The MAGIC of Synergy."

- FREE group instruction became a value-added feature designed to generate parent support for the program. The content focused on performance skills (Master Classes), Theory Classes related to the Piano Adventures Curriculum, Ear Training & Reading Skills (Basic Musicianship), and Exam Preparation.

- With so many students from the community coming to me who were struggling to learn and do well on RCM exams, I wanted to create solutions, and so I focused on addressing areas of weakness that I saw occurring regularly.

- I chose an established curriculum (Faber Piano Adventures) that was the most sequential and comprehensive of any that I had ever seen, and insisted that all of my teachers use it.

- In response to the problems that were coming to my attention on a regular basis, I established a policy that no curriculum books were to be skipped, no parts of the books were to be skipped, and no grade levels were to be skipped.

- I set up a strategy that involved dividing instruction time between myself and my staff so that I could monitor student progress and ensure that all students were progressing as expected.

- I began having workshops and communicating with my teachers to ensure that my expectations were being met.

- I introduced a parent seminar as an orientation strategy, and followed up with one-month program at a very special rate called *Lesson Launcher* for the purpose of demonstrating the enormous power of my Achievers Programs. The various components such as The Powerful PRAISE Techniques, and including "The MAGIC of Synergy" make-up "The Talent CAN Be Taught System". Writing the book and creating a brochure also both help to provide parent orientation.

An Insightful Conversation with an Independent Teacher

Not too long after starting this program, a friend who was also an independent private music teacher discovered my RCM First Class Honours guarantee and asked how I could possibly guarantee that. I replied, "Well, I know what it takes, and I make sure they do it." She may have thought my response was arrogant, and it certainly was a very short answer to a rather complex challenge, but I was simply stating the basic facts that characterized my new Achievers Programs.

**The key to success is knowing what it takes
and making sure it happens.**

I chose to accept responsibility for my students' progress. But at the same time, I did fully understand where she was coming from. Her view was the traditionally accepted view of many independent private teachers who use strategies that I now refer to as the failing traditions.

She happened to be a very dedicated teacher, but like most other independent private teachers, many of her students received no more than a one-hour private lesson each week, because that is the most widely accepted tradition. Of course, this leaves the next six days entirely to the students to teach themselves. And so, the dropout rate of these students is about the same as almost all students who embark on this path. As a result, every few years, like all private music teachers, studios, or students who use this formula, there is almost a complete turnover of clients, with relatively few progressing through and enjoying success in the more advanced levels.

When students don't do well, the assumption is that the student either didn't practice enough, or lacks sufficient talent. The truth, however, is that when students become frustrated by the slow rate of progress that results from trying to learn exclusively through independent practice six out of seven days a week, eventually both they and their families give up rather than continue to struggle with increasing hassles over practicing. And, most critical to the goal of achieving success, with only 30-minutes per week of expert teaching support, students never have an opportunity to develop any of the synergy that results from accelerated learning and the motivation that comes from success, because the lesson schedule is simply too infrequent to allow it to happen.

Most independent private teachers also don't offer supplemental group lessons as a value added feature to ensure special skill development. They believe that this is not a practical use of their time. So, the traditional thinking of the failing traditions is about traditional practices, traditional price structures, and in the end, except for a very few, traditionally declining results and growing frustration that leads almost always to students quitting within a few months or years.

Value Added Features

One of the hallmarks of our Achievers Programs is the value-added feature bonuses that are included in the price of private music lessons.

Curriculum Theory Classes

For beginner piano students, there are FREE supervised work periods for completing theory exercises that are a part of the comprehensive curriculum of study.   This accomplishes two main objectives.   First, valuable private lesson time is not wasted, and second, the supervised classroom setting helps ensure that the exercises are completed.   While this is basically an independent work period, a teacher is available to help ensure that students understand what they are doing, and to check their work.   This is an important service, because it is something that many parents with insufficient background training in music are unable to do to help their own children.

Performance Master Classes

All students are encouraged to perform, and periodically are invited to attend FREE Master Performance Classes.   The objective is to provide an opportunity for students to experience performing for each other, usually as a rehearsal prior to performing at a studio recital, local festival, or an RCM exam.   It also serves as a training ground, coaching students on important strategies for performing publicly.

Basic Musicianship Classes

The process of developing a musical ear takes time, and includes a variety of activities, including singing, listening, studying musical style, and learning how to take musical dictation, to name just a few.

The Lesson Launcher™

This program allows parents to register students for three hours per week for a single month in what is essentially our premium Achievers Program without the additional free group instruction.   At the end of this time, students and parents will have experienced the amazing results of the program, and will then be able to make a more informed decision on what program they wish to register for going forward. Those who attend the Talent CAN Be Taught Seminar also receive a special extra discount if they choose to register for our Lesson Launcher. I offer this discount for attending the seminar because I understand that parents must be fully informed of the benefits in order to be able to support and commit to the strategy. And ultimately, that will lead to the success which everyone really wants.

Summary – Making Decisions

Few children have either the knowledge or the maturity to make wise, informed decisions for their own music education. Parents must be responsible to make these decisions for them.

Some parents who register young children for music lessons, allow their children to make the choice of instrument. And, since the children have no idea about what is involved in learning the instrument or what would be an appropriate choice, poor decisions are made that lead to the student losing interest and quitting. The reality is that few if any young children have either the knowledge or the maturity to make wise, informed decisions for their own music education. Children might choose an instrument because they like the colour of the instrument, for example, or saw someone playing it. And, when I hear someone say that they have come to register for music lessons, for example, because their five year old wants to learn to play drums, I usually take the opportunity to advise the parent about the FREE Talent CAN Be Taught Seminars that we offer. This way I know that parents will be able to make more informed decisions and gain the greatest benefit from the money that they plan to invest in their children's music education. And so, as it is unlikely that young children will have the benefit of understanding the keys to success in private music education that this book presents, it is necessary for those who do understand to accept responsibility for making these important decisions.

Please visit: www.talentcanbetaught.com

Epilogue

Building for the Future:
Continuing the Legacy by Training Teachers

If you nurture others but allow them to become dependent on you, you're really hurting them, not helping them
— John C. Maxwell, author

In keeping with my goal to continually improve private music education first and foremost for the benefit of students, but in a broader sense, to create a better legacy to replace the failing traditions, my most recent innovation is the development of two new Achievers programs with a view to the future.

Student Acceleration Program

The first of these ideas attempts to address the desire of many to achieve results more quickly without compromising any aspects of the program which we have been dedicated to creating. This gifted student or acceleration strategy seeks to encourage all students but especially those demonstrating fast growth of music skills to supplement their learning with additional and more advanced repertoire. At the same time we ensure that they do not neglect any of the proven steps to success or sacrifice any of the governing principles that are contributing to the success of our Achievers programs. This strategy will prepare students for additional performance opportunities and enable them to participate sooner and at a more advanced level in competitive festivals.

Teacher Apprentice Program

The gifted student or acceleration program works together with and leads into our second new initiative which is the introduction of teacher apprentice training. It is a well-known educational principle that teaching serves to re-enforce and bring into better focus an understanding of lessons learned. This program is designed for students approaching high school age and beyond who are entering the upper levels of music training. In addition to all of the benefits of the acceleration strategy, the apprentices will also receive teacher training and teaching assignments. These enable them first to earn high school community service credits by assisting younger, novice level students participating in some of our FREE value added bonus programs, after which they will be given paid teaching assignments, and eventually significant leadership opportunities within The Talent CAN Be Taught System.

Summary

These strategies are designed to help and encourage students to set no limits on their own personal paths to excellence, as well as to participate in the ongoing development of a new legacy for excellence in private music education in general, and the Talent CAN Be Taught system that, it is my hope, will eventually replace the failing traditions.

About the Author

Stephen Riches is an experienced teacher, conductor, pianist, accompanist, vocal coach, adjudicator, arranger, and composer. He is a member of the Ontario College of Teachers, holding Bachelor of Music and Bachelor of Education degrees from the University of Toronto, and an ARCT in Piano Performance.

In 1977, he was winner of Canada's elite Dr. Heinz Unger Conducting Competition. This is a talent that he had been encouraged to develop during the years studying with renowned Canadian pianist and composer, Clifford Poole. Over the years, Stephen has performed both as a piano soloist and conductor with a number of community orchestras, as well as for numerous special charitable events. He is also frequently in demand as a piano accompanist for concerts, festivals, and auditions, in addition to which he has conducted many Broadway shows and operettas. In 1993, he was Founding Music Director and Conductor of the Pickering Philharmonic Orchestra, and later the Festival Players Philharmonic Society, providing memorable concerts in local Durham communities for many years.

Stephen's experience in education extends to teaching in both the private and public school systems, where for many years he has directed bands, choirs, and orchestras in both elementary and secondary school panels. He has also served as an adjudicator for music festivals, and has been a guest presenter of professional activity day music workshops for secondary school teachers. He continues to regularly present seminars and workshops on a variety of topics relating especially to music and education. In recent years, he has also been providing leadership in Christian music ministries, especially working with contemporary praise and worship teams, in addition to starting his own private music studio. And now, adding author to his long list of credits with "Talent CAN Be Taught," Stephen has been implementing the successful strategies contained in his book to the great benefit of his students.

Please visit: www.talentcanbetaught.com

Notes